QUANTUM HUMAN DESIGN EVOLUTION GUIDE

2024

USING SOLAR TRANSITS TO DESIGN YOUR YEAR

KAREN CURRY PARKER

Edited by Debby Levering
Cover Design by: Kristina Edstrom

HUMANDESIGN
— PRESS —

An Imprint for GracePoint Publishing (www.GracePointPublishing.com)

GracePoint Matrix, LLC
624 S. Cascade Ave, Suite 201
Colorado Springs, CO 80903
www.GracePointMatrix.com
Email: Admin@GracePointMatrix.com

SAN # 991-6032

A Library of Congress Control Number has been requested and is pending.

ISBN: (Paperback) 978-1-961347-43-4
eISBN: 978-1-961347-44-1

Books may be purchased for educational, business, or sales promotional use.
For bulk order requests and price schedule contact:
Orders@GracePointPublishing.com

Other Books and Resources by Karen Curry Parker

Abundance by Design

Human Design Workbook

Inside the Body of God

Introduction to Quantum Human Design™ 2nd Edition

Quantum Human Design™ Activation Cards

*Quantum Human Design™ Activation Cards
Companion Book*

QHD Quantum Activation Card Deck (iPhone App)

Human Design and the Coronavirus

The Quantum Human: The Evolution of Consciousness and the Solar Plexus Mutation in Human Design

Understanding Human Design

Quantum Human Design™ Evolution Guide 2023

Purpose by Design

Encyclopedia of Quantum Human Design

Follow Karen and Quantum Human Design on social media

@KarenCurryParker

CONTENTS

DEDICATION

To all my students, Quantum Human Design™ Specialists, and Quantum Alignment Practitioners: Thank you for trusting me to be your teacher. Thank you for sharing the gift of Who You Truly Are with the world. I am because you are. I love you!

INTRODUCTION

This book is a weekly guide designed to give you a deliberate way to harness the energy of the Sun and the Moon to support you in creating what you want in your life.

Quantum Human Design™ is a collection of cross-cultural, ancient, and modern archetypes. An archetype is a pattern of thought or symbolic image that is derived from the past collective experience of humanity.

We experience all of the archetypes in the Human Design chart, either from our own unique chart, our relationships, or through the planetary transits. In other words, we all have all of the chart, but we experience the archetypes of the chart differently depending on the unique configuration of our individual chart.

The colored in or "defined" elements in your Human Design chart tell you which archetypes you carry. The defined elements in your chart are part of what you must conquer to bring your gifts into the world. These energies represent your soul curriculum or what you're here to learn over the course of your life.

The white or "open" elements in your Human Design chart tell you a lot about what you are here to learn from others and from the world. You will experience these archetypes in a variety of different ways depending on who you are with and what energies are transiting in the celestial weather. The undefined elements of your chart represent the themes you are designed to explore through your relationships with others and your interactions with the world.

Over the course of a calendar year, the Sun moves through all 64 of the Human Design gates. The Human Design gates contain the energy code for 64 core human archetypes. As the Sun moves through an archetype, it lights up for everyone on the planet, creating a theme for the week and we all deal with these weekly themes. Even if the theme doesn't impact your chart deeply, it will impact the charts of the people around you. The gift of the solar transit is that it gives you an opportunity to work deliberately with all 64 of these core human archetypes and to consciously focus on living the highest expression of these energies in your daily life. The solar transits also bring you creative energies that help you meet the goals you set for yourself each year.

The Moon in Human Design represents the energy of what drives us. In traditional astrology, the new Moon phase and the full Moon phase represent bookend energies that mark the beginning and the end of a monthly creative cycle.

The new Moon helps us set the intention for our goals for the month. The full Moon supports us in releasing any energies, beliefs, or blocks that are hindering the completion of our goals.

Lunar and Solar eclipses are also bookends that mark beginnings and endings. The work we do in between can be powerful, and both internal as well as external. Eclipse energy represents cycles that support us in aligning more deeply with the bigger goals in life and support us in breaking free from habits and patterns that keep us from growing and expanding.

To learn more about the transits and how they affect your personal Human Design chart and your energy visit here:

http://www.freehumandesignchart.com

HOW TO USE THIS BOOK

The *2024 Quantum Human Design Evolution Guide* is a workbook with a weekly writing assignment, affirmations, and Emotional Freedom Techniques (EFT) setup phrases. If you are not a fan of journaling, feel free to contemplate the prompts in whatever way works for you. You may walk with them, meditate on them, or even discuss them with your friends.

I am excited to share with you updated Quantum Human Design™ language. Over the years it has become obvious to me the vocabulary in Human Design is in need of an upgrade in response to evolutionary shifts and with respect to new research that shows how the language we use is so powerful it can even change your DNA.

I hope you enjoy the new language!

The Quantum Human Design gates and planets have a challenge associated with them. This is what you must master to get the most out of the movement of the Sun which occurs approximately every six days. Before you complete the writing assignment, read the challenge for each gate and contemplate what you need to do to get the most out of each of the weekly archetypes.

Included are the Earth transits to help you explore how to nurture and ground yourself each week. The energy of the Earth helps you stay aligned and supported so that you can better accomplish the themes highlighted by the Sun. In addition to the Solar contemplations, you'll find a short contemplation or exercise to help you stay grounded and nurtured during the week, based on the theme highlighted by the Earth.

This year we've also added Mercury Retrograde cycles. You'll learn about these key "cosmic pauses" that invite us to go inward and realign with our voice, our message, and our relationships.

The Emotional Freedom Technique is a powerful energy psychology tool that has been scientifically proven to change your emotional, mental, and genetic programming to help you express your highest potential. Each week you may work with a specific EFT setup phrase to help you clear any old energies you may be carrying related to the archetype of the week. Learn more about how to use EFT here: https://quantumhumandesign.com/quantum-human-design-resources/

You will also find exercises for each new Moon, full Moon, Solar eclipse, and Lunar eclipse complete with a writing/contemplation assignment and affirmation. You'll be guided in working with the theme of the Lunar cycles and eclipses so that you can make the most of these powerful energy cycles.

Every Human Design year gives us a 365-day creative cycle that supports us in releasing what no longer serves us, allows us to consciously increase our creative energy, grow, and evolve with the support of the stars.

May you have a prosperous and joyful 2024!

THE THEME OF THE YEAR
2024: Alignment versus Willpower

Welcome to 2024!

This year promises to be a year that might feel like we're completing a final exam or defending a dissertation. We've been studying, practicing, and preparing for 2024 since the planet Uranus entered the sign of Taurus in 2019. This is the year where we must walk our talk and take the aligned actions necessary to prepare for the future.

The celestial weather sets the stage for our evolution. The planets are not at fault. We are not hapless victims of a planetary program that "causes" human destruction and misalignment. The planets simply highlight key archetypal themes that give us structural elements and a plot outline for our story. It's up to us to decide what we do with these themes.

To really understand what's up on the planet this year, we have to review some of the critical celestial themes that have been influencing us over the past five years. Uranus in Taurus, starting in 2019, is setting the stage for massive upheaval and growth. All systems eventually outgrow their capacity to fulfill their original intention. When systems reach the end of their lifespan, they come apart, creating room for something new, something more effective. Uranus in Taurus is a catalyst for massive change on a systemic level. Old systems that no longer serve the greater good, such as the health care system, the economic system, the government system and more, are subject to being stretched and stressed as a result of outgrowing their capacity, creating a cycle of disruption.

Disruption is a natural part of growth and evolution. When our values change and we reach the limits of our growth, the old ways of doing things have to fall apart. In a way, this is a symptom of our souls calling for expansion. We've outgrown our old personal and collective narratives. We have to let our old story—our old identity—come apart to make room for a new story.

The cycles of expansion that we're facing can be personal and also collective. If you take a moment and think back to May of 2019 and then reflect on where you are right now, you'll realize that your life is probably pretty different.

COVID arrived shortly after Uranus entered Taurus. In Human Design, it is taught that pandemics start when the Sun shines on Gate 44, the Gate of Truth. This Gate brings us a theme of releasing the patterns of the past so that we can bring ourselves into greater alignment with integrity. COVID forced us to reevaluate our values and to redefine what's really valuable. It also brought us a powerful reminder that, even though we may be far apart on the globe, our actions impact each other profoundly.

Our experience with COVID placed an enormous amount of stress on our health care system, our economy, and the education system and even brought attention to the inequity of gender and gender roles in the home as families shifted to at-home education with women bearing the bulk of the responsibility of supporting the children and simultaneously running a household and, often, continuing to also work at their jobs or run their own businesses.

Our values shifted during this time. Many people experienced tragic loss. Businesses closed or had to evolve how they deliver their services. We are still in the midst of an epidemic of "quiet quitting" while our economy continues to recover. Many families realized the importance of time together and began to make changes to reflect a quieter, less materialistic lifestyle. We certainly learned that the effects of a singular event anywhere on the planet have the capacity to affect us all in profound ways.

Disruption is always a symptom of growth, our higher selves calling us forward toward something better. Disruption forces us to redefine who we are and begin the process of establishing a new identity, a new story about who we are and who we are becoming. We're vulnerable when we are disrupted. While part of us knows that we must keep our momentum moving forward, we grieve and long to go back to how things used to be. When we don't manage our growth with awareness and intention, we run the risk of getting stuck in frustration, fear, anger, bitterness, and disappointment. We get trapped in our grief, keeping our emotions trapped while we long to go back…

Cycles of disruption can trigger a sense of deep loss. We are personally and collectively going through the five stages of grief: denial, anger, bargaining, depression, and acceptance. The surge in divisive politics and, in particular, the surge in orthodox and conservative movements are all societal responses to loss and the embodiment of a desire to go back to how things used to be.

But you can never go back. The person we were pre-disruption is gone. They will never return. The challenge is to integrate the blessings and the lessons and use disruption as a way to intentionally clarify what we want next. We are healing from the pain of the past and simultaneously deciding what's in front of us that's worth running towards.

This has been true these past few years both on a personal and a collective level. We have been in a cycle of liminality, a threshold space where we have to decide how to go forward because we can no longer return to the past. The question is how will we move forward? Will we tell stories of our wounding and craft an identity rooted in our brokenness, or will we find the threads of what IS working and weave those threads into a new and better story?

We all know that we are unique. That deep awareness of our uniqueness pulses in our veins yearning for us to express it out into the world. The quest for our authentic identity has been loud and amplified these past few years. We all know we are unique. That deep awareness of our uniqueness pulses in our veins yearning for us to express it out into the world. We mistakenly think our brokenness sets us apart or that our pain differentiates us from others. But what really sets us apart is our brilliance. We are all broken in the same way. What makes us unique is all the different ways we are brilliant.

Resilience is the theme of 2024. How do we show up for a rapidly changing world and stay fluid, capable of pivoting and adjusting to the challenges and opportunities that reveal themselves? To stay resilient in 2024, we must proclaim our brilliance and have the courage to protect it and use it as the light that shines our way forward. It takes more courage to be brilliant than it does to stay broken.

The Nodes

The Nodes represent the *plot outline* in the story of the year ahead. The Nodal pairs reflect how we mature and evolve over the days ahead and what challenges we must overcome in order to fulfill the potential of this year.

If we look to the Nodes to define the primary themes of this year, we see that the Nodes are laying out a soul curriculum of helping us learn to trust the wisdom of the heart, to draw our energy from the spark that is ignited by our alignment versus harnessing our willpower, and to continue improving by cultivating a consistent practice that supports strengthening our creative skills.

Creativity in this case isn't about glitter, paint, and interpretive dancing. It's about our ability to respond intentionally and deliberately to what's needed in the moment. The moments ahead may be volatile and highly fluid, requiring us to be facile and adept at using our creativity to pivot and stay aligned as the key to knowing where to take the "next right step" in moving forward.

We're also learning to manage our response to fear and to stay out of reactivity and old patterns so that we can move forward with faith and confidence. The Nodes instruct us to dig deep and find the courage to move forward because the call of our purpose and what we're running towards is stronger than the call to run away from our fear.

The Nodes highlight gates of the heart chakra (the Will Center and the G-Center) for most of the year, reminding us that we create better when we're in alignment with our purpose. Brute force and will power are both finite and unsustainable. This theme of will versus purpose plays out in multiple layers of the celestial weather for all of 2024.

A good contemplative question to ask if you find yourself wandering around in the "Worst Case Scenario" rabbit hole this year is "How can I retrain my focus on what I want and need?"

January—May 11, 2024

We start the year with the South Node highlighting Gate 51, the Gate of Initiation, and the North Node highlighting Gate 57, the Gate of Instinct. We are beginning the year with a cycle of disruption, shock, and initiation that inspires us to deepen our connection to our purpose and to Source. New ideas are sparked by massive change, and we begin the process of building something new—something better—that leads us into the future. With this energy, we run the risk of being afraid of the future. The antidote is to stay connected to our faith and a vision of what we're building towards.

May 11—July 20, 2024

On May 11, the Nodes shift to the South Node highlighting Gate 21, the Gate of Self-Regulation, and the North Node highlighting Gate 48, the Gate of Wisdom. We are invited to explore how to structure our lives so that we are sustainable. We are encouraged to rest, nurture ourselves and create an inner and outer environment that supports us in becoming more self-generous for the sake of strengthening and deepening our capacity and to build the resources we have to share with others. The more we value ourselves, the more we trust ourselves and value who we are and the unique gifts that only we can share with the world. We relax in knowing that we are prepared for what's ahead. This transit forces us to have to come eyeball to eyeball with ourselves and any perception of inadequacy. We are being pushed to take action, even if we think we're not ready. Hint: We are.

July 20—December 4, 2024

The South Node now moves to Gate 17, the Gate of Anticipation, and the North Node moves to Gate 18, the Gate of Realignment. It is worth noting that we are not only dealing with the challenge of harnessing purpose versus will, but we're also dealing with how to manage our fears with both Gate 48 from the previous nodal cycle and Gate 18 in this cycle being Splenic Gates. The combination of Gate 17 and 18, gives us the perfect shadow effect of feeling worried and allowing our worry to cause us to react and to hold us back from taking aligned action. In the high expression of these energies, we are open to new possibilities, expanding our thinking and waiting for the right time for the next right step to reveal itself.

It's also worth noting that Gate 18 is also a gate that brings with it the theme of practice and practicing. Gate 21 from the previous cycle reminded us that we need to stay practiced at regulating ourselves. Gate 18 gives us the theme of practice as a path to improvement. This year, the more we practice, the more we strengthen our capacity to bend, flow, and adapt to how the path unfolds, even if it seems unexpected and uncertain.

December 4, 2024

In our final Nodal cycle, the South Node moves to highlight Gate 25, the Gate of Spirit, and the North Node moves to Gate 46, the Gate of Embodiment. We finish up the year back in the heart chakra exploring our relationship with our higher purpose and how to best embody this purpose. After a year of twists, turns, and initiations in our personal and collective stories, we are in need of healing and aligning. For many of us, this cycle represents a time to literally get on our knees and pray for clarity and support. For those of us who have heeded the curriculum of the year and have discovered the spark of energy that comes when we align first and then act, this cycle can be a surge forward: a time when we embody and materialize the fulfillment of our purpose and our path.

Uranus, Neptune, and Pluto—The Outer Planets and Global Themes

The outer planets also offer us deep insights into the plot outline of the year. These slower-moving planets set the tone and the direction for where we're headed and outline key archetypal themes that support us in our collective, global, and personal evolution.

Uranus

Uranus, the cosmic disruptor, brings the energy of the unexpected. Uranus loves to disrupt the status quo, bringing us unexpected shifts and changes that, ultimately, force us to grow.

Uranus continues its transit through the sign of Taurus until April, 2026. We start the year with Uranus highlighting Gate 23, the Gate of Transmission, until June 7 when it moves to highlight Gate 8, the Gate of Fulfillment. Both of these energies are what is called "mutative" energy in Human Design. Mutative energies bring evolution, growth, and the new. We are discovering how our relentless commitment to our authentic self-expression, and trusting our own knowingness invites us to restructure the way we create our lives. We can no longer compromise on who we are in every arena of our lives. This puts tension on any old agreements you may have made from an inauthentic position. Time to be honest and move on or renegotiate.

These questions have been playing out in the arena of our finances in particular. Uranus in Taurus shakes up collective structures that are out of sync with our evolution and growth, dismantling systems that no longer serve higher ideals of sustainability, justice, and equity.

We have learned that change and transformation are inevitable and that, when we trust ourselves and our own connection to Source, we know what we need to know when we need to know it and we know what we need to do next. The challenge is that not everyone has been doing the same work as you. Gate 23 reminds us to wait to share what we know with the people who truly value our knowing and the wisdom we have, and to not waste our energy trying to convince others who are not ready. This is extremely transformative energy that, when shared with the right people, dramatically transforms what we think is possible.

The revolutions that are transpiring are not about convincing and dragging others forward into their evolution if they're not ready. It's about quietly living in alignment and modeling what alignment and creative fulfillment looks like.

Neptune

Neptune, the planet that brings us spiritual growth, starts the year off continuing to highlight Gate 36, the Gate of Exploration. This planetary curriculum gives us a gentle reminder to hold a vision and sustain it with an aligned frequency of emotional energy and to wait to bring that vision into form only when the timing is right. We are learning to stretch the boundaries and limits of the human story. This Gate is a place where patterns are shattered by creating and, ultimately, exploring something different and new. We are breaking free from a predictable future that we've outgrown and we're moving forward with gusto.

The challenge here is to not move forward without right timing and alignment. This is emotional energy and it's often hard to see the truth and what is actually being shattered. Without awareness this gate can bring chaos. But chaos is often the precursor to things being reorganized and, ultimately, transformed.

On April 10, Neptune moves to highlight Gate 25, the Gate of Spirit, inviting us to trust the process and to continue to commit to our higher purpose and a higher vision. When things seem confusing or hard to understand, Neptune promises clarity when we let go and connect with Source. We are part of a bigger picture unfolding. Even if it feels chaotic in the moment, we are realigning towards something that better represents the fulfillment of the new human story.

Pluto

Pluto, the planet of expansion and transformation, highlights Gate 60, the Gate of Conservation, all year, reminding us that progress is best built on what is already working. We are reminded that if we're going to innovate, we need to be mindful of not alienating everyone and tossing everything out. We need to carefully explore what is working and grow it by being grateful for it, no matter how small it may seem.

The temptation with this transit is that we can long to go back to how things were before and may continue to see a swing back toward outdated ideals. These seemingly backward slides won't last as the Nodes remind us that there is no going back, tempting as it may be. The only way to grow is to shift our focus in the direction we want to be heading. You can't un-evolve!

The shadow of this energy is a continued resurgence in conservatism, extremism, and orthodoxy all seeking to control our inevitable evolution. Eventually we all realize we can't go back, and the only way forward is to adapt, pivot, and ultimately transform. Be prepared for people to be resistant to change and know that sometimes you have to meet people where they are in order to be able to reassure them that forward, is indeed, a very fine direction.

The movement of these three major celestial players gives us a continued storyline of tension and potential division. The old is pitted against the new. For all of us to move forward in a significant and transformational way, we have to be patient and wait for everyone to catch up. Conservatism is simply a symptom of change. To quote the late Buckminster Fuller, "You never change things by fighting the existing reality. To change something, build a new model that makes the existing model obsolete."

Saturn and Jupiter

We finish up our overview of the major planetary movements by taking a closer look at Saturn and Jupiter. These two planets dance together in the sky, revealing the relationship between the work we must do and the rewards available to us when we do the work.

Over the course of this year, Jupiter highlights the following gates:

January 1–Gate 27, The Gate of Accountability

February 4–Gate 24, The Gate of Blessings

March 12–Gate 2, The Gate of Allowing

April 8–Gate 23, The Gate of Transmission

May 3–Gate 8, The Gate of Fulfillment

May 26–Gate 20, The Gate of Patience

June 20–Gate 16, The Gate of Zest

July 16–Gate 35, The Gate of Experience

August 17–Gate 45, The Gate of Distribution

December 1–Gate 35, The Gate of Experience

Saturn highlights the following gates:

January 1–Gate 55, The Gate of Faith

January 26–Gate 37, The Gate of Peace

March 13–Gate 63, The Gate of Curiosity

May 5–Gate 22, The Gate of Surrender

August 26–The Gate 63, The Gate of Curiosity

What these two celestial friends show us is that this year we must deepen and strengthen our faith so that we may act in alignment with our positive expectations. This is crucial if we're going to stay aligned with sufficiency, peace, and possibility. The rewards of using intentional creativity and being deliberate are being in sync with right timing and access to the energy necessary to take aligned action when the timing is right, dramatically increasing our productivity and our abundance.

This is a year that promises to test us. It will be a year with the potential for tremendous creativity, energy, and transformation if we stay in the habit of using alignment and purpose to keep us moving forward. To tap into the energy available, you must let go of all stories of limitation and lack that you may have been allowing to block you from building toward what you truly want. Faith, self-care, and consciously crafting an inner and outer environment that supports you in continuing to stay aligned with your purpose and the full expression of your authentic self, is essential to staying resilient and being able to pivot during this time of massive change.

Take care of your body, your mind, and your spirit so that you stay in a powerful state of receptivity that allows you to know what you need to know and to act on what you need to act on when the time is right.

Not everyone is going to get and understand what is happening. Many around you will feel that they are in crisis or chaos. The most powerful and loving gift you can give the world is to keep actualizing your own abundance and potential. Your role this year is to anchor and deepen the foundation upon which you are building an abundant and sustainable life. The more you embody this, the more you can better help and lead others in due time.

It's going to be a great year!

From my heart to yours,
Karen

2024 ECLIPSE SEASON

Eclipses serve as celestial checkpoints. An eclipse is a high-octane celestial event that helps illuminate our karmic path, but just as these cosmic events can be visually striking, eclipses can also be a bit dramatic. Astrologically speaking, they speed up time. They open new doors by slamming others shut, so we often find abrupt and sudden shifts occurring during eclipses.

Though the shifts can be jarring, they can help us by speeding up the inevitable. If you've been dragging your feet, an eclipse will be sure to give you that extra push (or shove) needed to take action. While the results can be shocking, remember that these celestial events simply expedite the inevitable—these events were going to happen eventually.

Understanding transits helps you consciously harness the power of the transit and use it to your advantage. This won't necessarily help you avoid the intensity of these catalytic celestial events, but it will help you influence the outcome and better regulate your response to them. Remember, you can't always control what happens in your life, but you always have control over what you do with these events.

During Solar eclipses, the Moon is directly between the Earth and Sun, where the Sun and the Moon are said to be in conjunction. For some time, the tiny Moon has the capability to block out the giant Sun and turn off the lights on Earth. This might shift our perspectives in life. Solar eclipses are said to take away fixed patterns and push us into unknown realms. Though this might cause upheaval in our lives, they are excellent growth promoters and powerful catalysts.

A Lunar eclipse is an astronomical event that occurs when the Moon moves into the Earth's shadow, causing the Moon to be darkened. Astrologically, a Lunar eclipse intensifies what needs to be brought to light in order for us to release, heal, align, or become aware of limits that block us from fulfilling our goals and dreams. This energy delivers a powerful opening to growth by helping us explore what needs to be seen and revealed in order for us to create with greater integrity.

This year we work primarily with eclipses on the Aries/Libra axis. We also get a sneak peek into our "next chapter" in September with our first eclipse on the Pisces/Virgo axis. The themes of the eclipse axis work hand in hand with the overarching astrological theme of the year, enhancing and deepening what aspect of our personal and collective stories we are evolving.

The Aries/Libra axis invites us into an inner dialogue that encourages us to be relentlessly authentic and even youthful or bold with our actions. Aries can be immature and headstrong and often needs to be tempered by the quest for balance highlighted by Libra. Again, we are asking ourselves how we can be honest about who we are and what we need and diplomatic about how we can get our needs met. We are exploring our needs and wants. We are becoming aware of any place where we perceive ourselves lacking and learning how to transform these perceptions into an awareness of where we are already abundant.

In September we get our first eclipse on the Pisces/Virgo axis. We are exploring improvement versus our discontent and looking at which patterns need to be disrupted and reordered so that we may create something new and better.

Below is a list of all the eclipse dates in this eclipse cycle, including the Human Design gates highlighted with each eclipse:

March 25–Penumbral Lunar Eclipse

Libra 5 degrees 7 minutes

Gate 18–The Gate of Realignment

April 8–Solar Eclipse

Aries 19 degrees 24 minutes

Gate 51–The Gate of Initiation

September 18–Lunar Eclipse

Pisces 25 degrees 41 minutes

Gate 36–The Gate of Exploration

October 2–Solar Eclipse

Libra 10 degrees 4 minutes

Gate 48–The Gate of Wisdom

You will find special eclipse contemplations in the 2024 Evolution Guide inserted on the dates of the 2024 eclipse events.

JANUARY 23, 2024
GATE 41: IMAGINATION

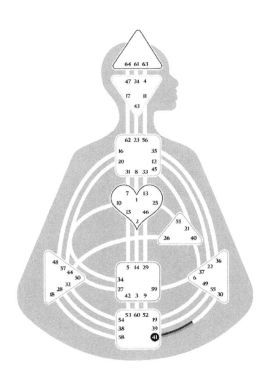

CHALLENGE:

To learn to use your imagination as a source of creative inspiration and manifestation. To experience the world and imagine more abundant possibilities. To stay connected to your creative fire.

JOURNAL QUESTIONS:

Do I own my creative power? How can I deepen my self-honoring of my creative power?

AFFIRMATION:

I am a creative nexus of inspiration for the world. My ideas and imaginations inspire people to think beyond their limitations. My ideas stimulate new possibilities in the world. I am a powerful creator; my creative thoughts, ideas, and inspirations set the stage for miracles and possibilities that will change the story of humanity.

EFT SETUP

Even though I am afraid my dreams won't come true, I deeply and completely love and accept myself.

EARTH:

Gate 31: Leadership

Explore this week what your place of service is. Who do you serve? What can you do to feel more empowered and influential in your life?

JANUARY 25, 2024
FULL MOON

 Leo 5 degrees, 14 minutes
Gate 31: The Gate of the Leader

Full Moon energy invites us to explore what we need to release and let go of in order to stay in alignment with our intentions.

This first full Moon in the Quantum Human Design year offers us an invitation into our creativity and our authentic self-expression, an incredible way to start the year! We're beginning a year-long quest to activate our natural creative power. We're looking at what we need to release in order to speak our truth and lead with integrity and heart and how to use our creative insights to find the elegant solutions to the challenges facing humanity.

The energy for leadership in the Quantum Human Design chart does not come from force or pushing. Leadership is natural, recognized, and compelling. We have more influence over our lives, our relationships, and the outer circumstances of our lives when we are aligned with our integrity.

Being radically honest about what you want and who you are and sharing this information without shame or hesitancy constitutes a key element of freedom. This level of unabashed alignment is compelling for others. People are drawn to you because you are carrying the energy of what they long for themselves. This isn't manipulation. You attract with your vibrational alignment and people can sense it.

This full Moon encourages radical honesty, but honesty that comes from the heart. It might feel brutal, but it has the capacity to realign the road ahead with the capacity to build genuine intimacy and effective solutions. Honesty is the foundation for sustainable and loving change.

Where do you need to be more honest and bolder in sharing who you are and what you need and want?

CHALLENGE:

To learn to lead as a representative of the people you lead. To cultivate a leadership agenda of service. To not let your fear of not being seen, heard, or accepted get in the way of healthy leadership. To learn to take your right place as a leader and not hide out.

OPTIMAL EXPRESSION:

The ability to listen, learn, hear, and serve the people you lead and to assume and value your right leadership position as the voice for the people you lead.

UNBALANCED EXPRESSION:

To push and seize leadership for the sake of personal gain or to be afraid to lead and not feel worthy of serving as a leader.

CONTEMPLATIONS:

How do I feel about being a leader? What does leading mean to me?

Am I comfortable leading?

Do I shrink from taking leadership?

What is my place of service?

Who do I serve?

What needs to be healed, released, aligned, and brought to my awareness for me to speak with an empowered voice?

AFFIRMATION:

I am a natural born leader. I serve at my highest potential when I am empowering others by giving them a voice and then serving their needs. I use my power to lead people to a greater expansion of who they are and to support them in increasing their abundance, sustainability, and peace, simply by being honest about who I am and what I need.

JANUARY 28, 2024
GATE 19: ATTUNEMENT

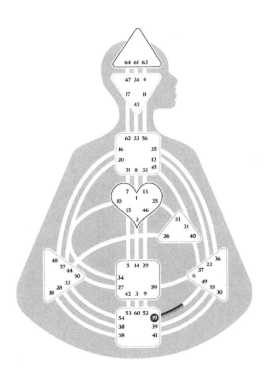

CHALLENGE:

To learn how to manage being a highly sensitive person and not let your sensitivity cause you to compromise what you want and who you are. To learn to keep your own resources in a sustainable state in order so that you have more to give. To not martyr yourself to the needs of others. To learn how to become emotionally intimate without being shut down or codependent.

JOURNAL QUESTIONS:

Am I emotionally present in my relationships?

Do I need to become more attuned to my own emotional needs and ask for more of what I want and need?

AFFIRMATION:

I am deeply aware of the emotional needs and energy of others. My sensitivity and awareness give me insights that allow me to create intimacy and vulnerability in my relationships. I am aware and attuned to the emotional frequency around me and I make adjustments to help support a high frequency of emotional alignment. I honor my own emotional needs as the foundation of what I share with others.

EFT SETUP:

Even though it is scary to open my heart, I now choose to create space for deep intimacy and love in my life, and I deeply and completely love and accept myself.

EARTH:

Gate 33: Retelling

What personal narratives are you telling yourself that might be keeping you stuck, feeling like a victim, or feeling unlovable? How can you rewrite these old stories?

FEBRUARY 3, 2024
GATE 13: NARRATIVE

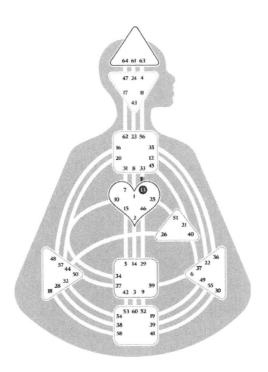

CHALLENGE:

To forgive the past and redefine who you are each and every day. To tell a personal narrative that is empowering and self-loving and reflects your value and your authentic self. To bear witness to the pain and narrative of others and offer them a better story that allows them to expand on their abundance and blessings.

JOURNAL QUESTIONS:

What stories about my life am I holding on to?

Do these stories reflect who I really am and what I want to create in my life?

What or who do I need to forgive in order to liberate myself to tell a new story?

What secrets or stories am I holding for others? Do I need to release them?

Write the true story of who I really am….

AFFIRMATION:

The story that I tell myself and the one I tell the world set the tone and direction for my life. I am the artist and creator of my story. I have the power to rewrite my story every day. The true story I tell from my heart allows me to serve my right place in the cosmic plan.

EFT SETUP:

Even though I'm afraid to speak my truth, I now share the truth from my heart, and trust that I am safe, and I deeply and completely love and accept myself.

EARTH:

Gate 7: Collaboration

Make a list of all the times your influence has positively directed and influenced leadership and important ideas. Stay open to working in teams or groups. Find support and encouragement in collaboration with others this week.

FEBRUARY 8, 2024
GATE 49: THE CATALYST

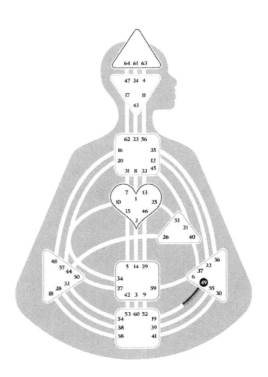

CHALLENGE:

To not quit prematurely or fail to start a necessary revolution in your life, to let go of unhealthy situations, relationships, or agreements that may compromise your value and worth.

JOURNAL QUESTIONS:

Am I holding on too long? Is there a circumstance and condition that I am allowing because I am afraid of the emotional energy associated with change?

Do I have a habit of quitting too soon? Do I fail to do the work associated with creating genuine intimacy?

What do I need to let go of right now to create room for me to align with higher principles?

AFFIRMATION:

I am a cosmic revolutionary. I am aligned with higher principles that support the evolution of humanity. I stand for peace, equity, and sustainability. I align with these principles, and I stand my ground. I do the work to create the intimacy necessary to share my values with others. I value myself and my work enough to only align with relationships that support my vital role.

EFT SETUP:

Even though my emotional response causes me to react and sometimes paralyzes me, I deeply and completely love and accept myself.

EARTH:

Gate 4: Possibility

Take time this week to contemplate new ideas and possibilities for your life. Dreaming and daydreaming support refining focus and alignment this week.

FEBRUARY 9, 2024
NEW MOON

 **Aquarius 20 degrees, 40 minutes**

Gate 49: The Gate of Catalyst

New Moon energy invites us to explore how we can deepen our alignment with our intentions and asks us to focus on what we want to grow and expand on in our lives.

This new Moon focuses heavily on the theme of beginnings. We can't have a new beginning without also sometimes bringing to completion the things that are keeping us from living in alignment with our value and values. With this potent energy, the Moon is asking us to begin a revolution in our lives in order to make room for something new and better, especially in our relationships.

The energy of this Moon may bring to your awareness aspects of your more intimate relationships that need to change in order for you to experience greater intimacy. This same energy can also sometimes give you clarity about ending cycles in your relationships that need to be brought to completion. The key question to explore is whether your relationships are rooted in common values and whether you feel valued in your more intimate partnerships. If not, it is time for a change. The changes you make with this new Moon will support you in experiencing deeper intimacy and partnership in the future.

There is a heavy focus with this new Moon energy on the power of Divine inspiration and the power of your imagination. Take some time to really dream about what you want and need in all of your relationships. The answers to your next right step will appear. Pay attention to your dreams and contemplations.

CHALLENGE:

To not quit prematurely. Holding on for longer than is healthy and to settle or compromise your value in situations, relationships, and with agreements that aren't worthy of you.

OPTIMAL EXPRESSION:

The ability to sense when it's time to stand in your value and set clear boundaries. The ability to inspire others to make expansive changes that embrace higher principles and a deeper alignment with peace and sustainability. The willingness to align with a higher value.

UNBALANCED EXPRESSION:

Quitting too soon as a way of avoiding intimacy. Compromising on your value and upholding agreements that no longer serve you. Creating drama and fighting for outdated values that no longer serve the higher good.

CONTEMPLATIONS:

Am I holding on too long?

Is there a circumstance and condition I am allowing because I fear the emotional energy associated with change?

Do I have a habit of quitting too soon?

Do I fail to do the work associated with creating genuine intimacy?

What do I need to let go of right now to create room to align with higher principles?

AFFIRMATION:

I am a Cosmic Revolutionary. I am aligned with higher principles that support the evolution of humanity. I stand for peace, equity, and sustainability. I align with these principles, and I stand my ground. I do the work to create the intimacy necessary to share my values with others. I value myself and my work enough to only align with relationships that support my vital role.

FEBRUARY 14, 2024
GATE 30: PASSION

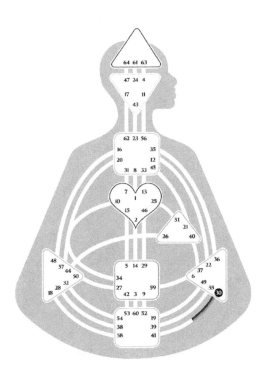

CHALLENGE:

To be able to sustain a dream or a vision without burning out. To know which dream to be passionate about. To not let passion overwhelm you and to wait for the right timing to share your passion with the world.

JOURNAL QUESTIONS:

What am I passionate about? Have I lost my passion?

How is my energy? Am I physically burned out? Am I burned out on my idea?

What do I need to do to sustain my vision or dream about what I am inspired to create in my life?

Do I have a dream or vision I am avoiding because I'm afraid it won't come true?

AFFIRMATION:

I am a passionate creator. I use the intensity of my passion to increase my emotional energy and sustain the power of my dream and what I imagine for life. I trust in the Divine flow, and I wait for the right timing and the right circumstances to act on my dream.

EFT SETUP:

Even though my excitement feels like fear, I now choose to go forward with my passion on fire, fully trusting the infinite abundance of the Universe, and I deeply and completely love and accept myself.

EARTH:

Gate 29: Devotion

Who would you be and what would you choose if you gave yourself permission to say no more often? What would you like to say no to that you are saying yes to right now? What obligations do you need to take off your plate right now?

FEBRUARY 19, 2024
GATE 55: FAITH

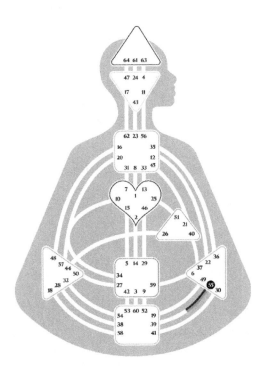

CHALLENGE:

To learn to trust Source. To know that you are fully supported. To become proficient in the art of emotional alignment as your most creative power.

JOURNAL QUESTIONS:

Do I trust that I am fully supported? What do I need to do to deepen that trust?

How can I align myself with abundant emotional energy? What practices or shifts do I need to make in my life to live and create in a more aligned way?

Do I surround myself with beauty? How can I deepen my experience of beauty in my life?

What do I have faith in now? What old gods of limitation do I need to stop worshipping?

Go on a miracle hunt. Take stock of everything good that has happened in my life. How much "magic" have I been blessed with?

AFFIRMATION:

I am perfectly and divinely supported. I know that all my needs and desires are being fulfilled. My trust in my support allows me to create beyond the limitation of what others think is possible and my faith shows them the way. I use my emotional energy as the source of my creative power. My frequency of faith lifts others and opens up a greater world of potential and possibility.

EFT SETUP:

Even though I struggle with faith and trusting Source, I deeply and completely love and accept myself.

EARTH:

Gate 59: Sustainability

Notice your energy this week. Are you feeling vital and sustainable? If not, what can you do to rest and renew yourself this week?

FEBRUARY 24, 2024
FULL MOON

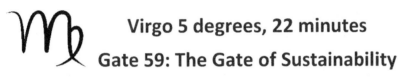 **Virgo 5 degrees, 22 minutes**

Gate 59: The Gate of Sustainability

Full Moon energy invites us to explore what we need to release and let go of in order to stay in alignment with our intentions.

This full Moon continues the theme of our new Moon earlier this month. We are contemplating our commitments, our connection, the degree of intimacy we are experiencing, and letting go of patterns, cycles, and even partnerships that are unsustainable.

We're also thinking about what we need to shift and change in order to be better partners and better providers to our loved ones, along with how to sustain ourselves so that we can build a better future. We are in a season of planting seeds that will eventually grow and yield what we want. We might not be able to see what we're planting, but our faith and our imagination are essential to building the template for what we want.

In the shadow of this energy, we feel lacking in some way. We're depleted and exhausted. This energy can lead to projection and even fighting if we don't have the energy to care for ourselves or for others. Gate 59 is one of the places where the potential energy for fighting and war live in the chart. Tread gently. Care for yourself first so that you can sustain yourself and others. Ask clearly for what you want and need. Be prepared for everyone to feel needy right now.

CHALLENGE:

To learn to make abundant choices that sustain you and, at the same time, others. To collaborate and initiate others into sustainable relationships from a place of sufficiency. To learn to share what you have in a sustainable way.

OPTIMAL EXPRESSION:

To trust in sufficiency and to know that when you create abundance, there is great fulfillment in sharing. To craft partnerships and relationships that sustain you and the foundation of your lives.

UNBALANCED EXPRESSION:

To feel like you have to fight or struggle to survive. To feel the need to penetrate others and force your rightness on them. To let fear of lack cause you to craft relationships and agreements that are unsustainable.

CONTEMPLATIONS:

Do you trust in your own abundance?

How do you feel about sharing what you have with others?

Are you creating relationship and partnership agreements that honor your work?

Do you have relationships and agreements that are draining you?

What needs to change?

How do you feel about being right?

Are you open to other ways of thinking or being?

Do you believe in creating agreements and alignments with people who have different values and perspectives?

AFFIRMATION:

The energy I carry has the power to create sufficiency and sustainability for all. I craft valuable alliances and agreements that support me in expanding abundance for everyone. I hold to higher principles and values rooted in my trust in sufficiency and the all-providing Source. Through my work and alignments, my blessings serve to increase the blessings of myself and others.

FEBRUARY 25, 2024
GATE 37: PEACE

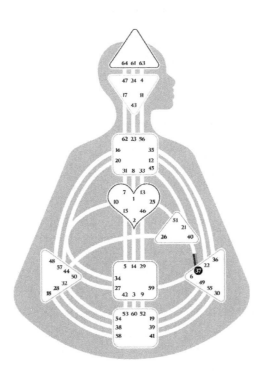

 CHALLENGE:

To find inner peace as the true source to outer peace. To not let chaos and outer circumstances knock you off your center and disrupt your peace.

 JOURNAL QUESTIONS:

What habits, practices, and routines do I have that cultivate my inner alignment with sustainable peace?

When I feel that my outer world is chaotic and disrupted, how do I cultivate inner peace?

What do I need to do to cultivate a peaceful emotional frequency?

AFFIRMATION:

I am an agent of peace. My being, aligned with peace, creates an energy of contagious peace around me. I practice holding a peaceful frequency of energy, and I respond to the world with an intention of creating sustainable peace.

EFT SETUP:

Even though I struggle to create peace and harmony in my life, I deeply and completely love and accept myself.

EARTH:

Gate 40: Restoration

We are grounded in rest, renewal, and reconnecting to our purpose this week. Take some time to truly nourish your body, mind, and spirit so that you have a full tank of energy reserves for the days ahead.

MARCH 1, 2024
GATE 63: CURIOSITY

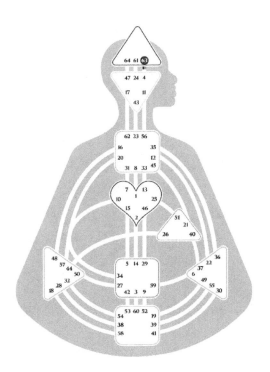

CHALLENGE:

To not let self-doubt and suspicion cause you to stop being curious.

JOURNAL QUESTIONS:

Am I curious about life?

Do I regularly allow myself to be curious about what else is possible in the world? In my life?

Do I doubt myself and my ideas?

What needs to happen for me to unlock my need to be right about an idea and to allow myself to dream of possibilities again?

AFFIRMATION:

My curiosity makes me a conduit of possibility thinking. I ask questions that stimulate imaginations. I allow the questions of my mind to seed dreams that stimulate my imagination and the imagination of others. I share my questions as an opening to the fulfillment of potential in the world.

EFT SETUP:

Even though I struggle with trusting myself, I now choose to relax and know that I know. I listen to my intuition. I abandon logic and let my higher knowing anchor my spirit in trust, and I deeply and completely love and accept myself.

EARTH:

Gate 64: Divine Transference

How can you embrace your dreams and stop judging them even if you don't know how to yet?

MARCH 7, 2024
GATE 22: SURRENDER

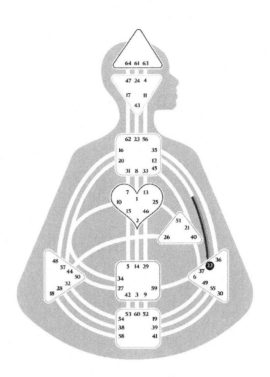

CHALLENGE:

To trust that your passions and deepest desires are supported by the universal flow of abundance. To have the courage to follow your passion and know that you will be supported. To learn to regulate your emotional energy so that you have faith that everything will unfold perfectly.

JOURNAL QUESTIONS:

Where am I denying my passion in my life? Where have I settled for less than what I want because I'm afraid I can't get what I want?

What do I need to do to fully activate my passion? What is one bold step towards my genius that I could take right now?

Do I trust the Universe? What do I need to do to deepen my trust?

Do I have a regular practice that supports me in sustaining a high frequency of emotional energy and alignment?

What needs to be healed, released, aligned, and brought to my awareness for me to deepen my faith?

AFFIRMATION:

I am a global change agent. I am inspired with passions that serve the purpose of transforming the world. I trust that my emotions and my passion will align me with faith and the flow of resources I need to fulfill my life purpose. When I let go and follow my passion, I am given everything I need to change the world.

EFT SETUP:

Even though it is hard to trust in my support, I now choose to trust anyway, and I deeply and completely love and accept myself.

EARTH:

Gate 47: Mindset

How can you cultivate more hope and optimism? This week practice enjoying all of your ideas for the sake of enjoying them without the expectation that you need to "figure out" how to turn those ideas into reality.

MARCH 10, 2024
NEW MOON

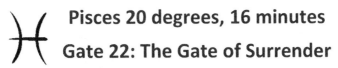

Pisces 20 degrees, 16 minutes
Gate 22: The Gate of Surrender

New Moon energy invites us to explore how we can deepen our alignment with our intentions and asks us to focus on what we want to grow and expand on in our lives.

We are still working with some intense Lunar energy that is pushing us to let go of the things we no longer have control over. The theme of this Moon offers us the opportunity to cultivate dreams that are bigger than our minds can figure out.

We have been sitting in a massive cycle of disruption and potential upheaval since the beginning of the year. Everything seems uncertain and unclear. There is tremendous potency in facing the unknown. We are forced to dream and imagine what we want, to "keep our eyes on the prize," and to keep moving forward as if it's all going to work out even if it feels uncomfortable right now.

Our capacity to create is increased exponentially when we trust that the solutions we are looking for are on their way, and we relax into this knowingness. This Moon reminds us to let go of thinking we need to figure out the answers and to surrender to the magic that we cultivate when we create with faith. Dream big and don't let your mind try to shrink your dreams just because you don't know how they're going to come true yet.

In the shadow of this Moon, we are scared. Our mindset is essential to keeping our hopes and dreams alive. Practice reminding yourself that it's all going to work out and that there are solutions available beyond what you can imagine. Try to play and keep your dopamine levels high during this Lunar transit.

CHALLENGE:

To trust that your passions and deepest desires are supported by the Universal flow of abundance. To have the courage to follow your passion and know you will be supported. To learn to regulate your emotional energy so you have faith that everything will unfold perfectly.

OPTIMAL EXPRESSION:

The grace to know that you are fully supported by the Universal flow of abundance and to pursue your passion and your unique contribution to the world no matter what. To trust that you will be given what you need when you need it in order to make your unique contribution to the world.

UNBALANCED EXPRESSION:

Fear that you are not supported. Holding back or stifling your passion because you think you can't afford to pursue it. Compromising, settling, or letting despair regulate your emotional energy causing the creative process to feel shut down or stuck.

CONTEMPLATIONS:

Where am I denying my passion in my life?

Where have I settled for less than what I want because I'm afraid I can't get what I want?

What do I need to do to fully activate my passion?

What is one bold step towards my genius that I could take right now?

Do I trust the Universe?

What do I need to do to deepen my trust?

Do I have a regular practice that supports me in sustaining a high frequency of emotional energy and alignment?

What needs to be healed, released, aligned, and brought to my awareness for me to deepen my faith?

AFFIRMATION:

I am a global change agent. I am inspired with passions that serve the purpose of transforming the world. I trust my emotions and my passions will align me with faith and the flow of resources I need to fulfill my life purpose. When I let go and follow my passion, I am given everything I need to change the world.

MARCH 13, 2024
GATE 36: EXPLORATION

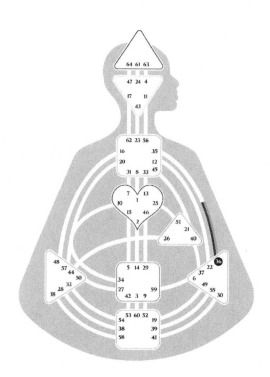

CHALLENGE:

To not let boredom cause you to leap into chaos. To learn to stick with something long enough to become skillful and to bear the fruits of your experience.

JOURNAL QUESTIONS:

How does boredom impact my life? What do I do when I feel bored? What can I do to keep myself aligned even when I'm bored?

What stories have I experienced that have shattered old patterns and expectations? How have my stories changed or inspired others?

What do I do to maintain or sustain emotional alignment? What do I need to add to my daily practice to amp up my emotional energy around my intentions?

AFFIRMATION:

My experiences and stories break old patterns and push the boundaries of the edge of what is possible for humanity. I defy the patterns and I create miracles through my emotional alignment with possibility. I hold my vision and maintain my emotional energy as I wait to bear the fruit of my intentions and my visions.

EFT SETUP:

Even though it is scary to be out of my comfort zone, I now choose to push myself into something new and more aligned with my truth, and I deeply and completely love and accept myself.

EARTH:

Gate 6: Impact

Contemplate how you feel about abundance. List all the different ways you have been abundantly supported in the past.

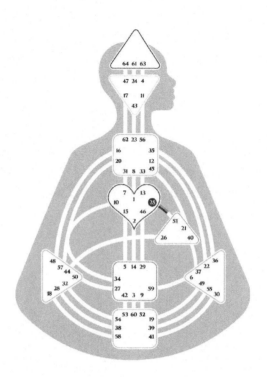

CHALLENGE:

To trust the Divine order in all of your life. To learn to connect with Source as the path to creating well-being in your life. To remember that your life serves an irreplaceable role in the cosmic plan. To honor that role and to live from it. To trust Source.

JOURNAL QUESTIONS:

Do I trust Source?

Do I have a regular practice that connects me to Source?

Do I know my life purpose?

Am I living true to my purpose?

How can I deepen my connection to my purpose?

AFFIRMATION:

I am an agent of the Divine. My life is the fulfillment of Divine order and the cosmic plan. When I am connected to Source, I serve my right place. I take up no more than my space and no less than my place in the world. I serve and through serving, I am supported.

EFT SETUP:

Even though in the past, I was afraid to follow my heart, I now choose to do what is right for me and know that I am fully supported, and I deeply and completely love and accept myself.

EARTH:

Gate 46: Embodiment

What do you need to do to better love and nurture your body? This week, spend some time in front of the mirror and ask your body what it needs to embody greater vitality.

MARCH 24, 2024
GATE 17: ANTICIPATION

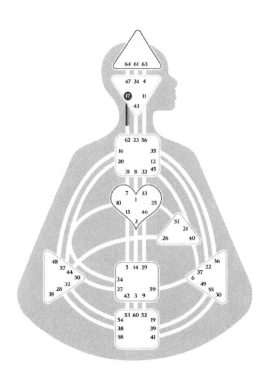

CHALLENGE:

To learn to share your thoughts about possibilities only when people ask for them. To not let doubt and suspicion keep you from seeing the potential of positive outcomes.

JOURNAL QUESTIONS:

What do I need to do to manage my insights and ideas so that they increase the options and potential of others?

How do I feel about holding back from sharing my insights until the timing is right?

What can I do to manage my need to share without waiting for the right timing?

What routines and strategies do I need to cultivate to keep my perspectives expanding and possibility-oriented?

How can I improve my ability to manage doubt and fear?

AFFIRMATION:

I use the power of my mind to explore possibilities and potential. I know the inspirations and insights that I have create exploration and experimentation that can inspire the elegant solutions necessary to skillfully control the challenges facing humanity.

EFT SETUP:

Even though I have a lot of ideas and thoughts to share, I trust that the insights I have to offer are too important to blurt out and I wait for the right people to ask, and I deeply and completely love and accept myself.

EARTH:

Gate 18: Realignment

This week explore where you need to add more joy to your life. Do you have any old stories you need to release around being right?

MARCH 25, 2024

FULL MOON/ PENUMBRAL LUNAR ECLIPSE

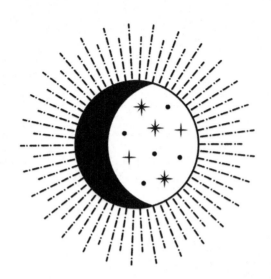

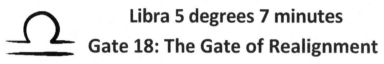

Libra 5 degrees 7 minutes

Gate 18: The Gate of Realignment

Full Moon energy invites us to explore what we need to release and let go of in order to stay in alignment with our intentions. Eclipse energy amplifies the intensity of the full Moon.

We are continuing our theme of being at the crossroads between something new and something old. When old systems outgrow their capacity, new systems emerge. There is a point in the growth process where we are standing with one foot in the midst of the old system and dealing with the breakdown of what no longer works, while at the same time standing with one foot in the midst of the new system and building towards the future. This is a theme we've been playing with since the end of 2023. We are letting go, making room and building all at the same time.

This cosmic design process can be messy. There's a lot of potential for tweaking, realigning, adjusting, and repairing as we build. Don't let the temporary adjustments to what you're building leave you feeling afraid that you'll never get it right or perfect. Make sure you stay connected to your joy as you build forward. It will drive you forward, even when it feels hard.

In the shadow of this energy, it might feel like everyone has opinions and criticisms. Trust yourself and your intuition. It's easy to quit when you hit a bump in the road. Stay the course, keep adjusting and keep moving forward. Think lean and release anything that might be blocking your path towards self-actualization.

CHALLENGE:

To learn to wait for right timing and right circumstances to offer your intuitive insights on how to fix or correct a pattern. To wait for right timing and the right reason to share your critique. To understand the purpose of realignment is to create more joy, not to be right.

OPTIMAL EXPRESSION:

To see a pattern that needs correcting and to wait for the right timing and circumstances to correct and align it. To serve joy.

UNBALANCED EXPRESSION:

To be critical. To share criticism without respect to the impact. To be more concerned with your own "rightness" than to assess whether your insight is actually adding more joy to the world.

CONTEMPLATIONS:

What does joy mean to me?

How do I serve it?

How do I cultivate joy in my own life?

How does it feel to be right about something and keep it to myself?

Do I need to release any old stories about needing to be right?

Do I trust my own insights?

Do I have the courage to share them when it's necessary?

AFFIRMATION:

I am a powerful force that realigns patterns. My insights and awareness give people the information they need to deepen their self-actualization and to experience greater joy. I serve joy and I align the patterns of the world to increase the world's potential for living in the flow of joy.

MARCH 30, 2024
GATE 21: SELF-REGULATION

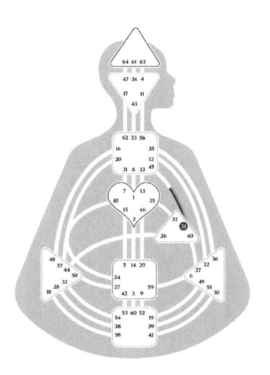

CHALLENGE:

To learn to let go. To become proficient at self-regulation. To release the need to control others and circumstances. To trust in the Divine and to know that you are supported. To know that you are worthy of support, and you don't have to overcompensate.

JOURNAL QUESTIONS:

Where do I need to release control in my life?

Do I trust the Universe?

Do I value myself? Do I trust that I will be supported in accordance with my value?

What do I need to do to create an internal and external environment of self-generosity?

What needs to be healed, released, aligned, and brought to my awareness for me to embrace my true value?

AFFIRMATION:

I am worthy of claiming, protecting, and defending my rightful place in the world. I create an inner and outer environment that is self-generous, and I regulate my environment to sustain a high frequency of alignment with my true value. I know that I am an irreplaceable and precious part of the cosmic plan and I create my life to reflect the importance of my right place in the world.

EFT SETUP:

Even though in the past I felt like I had to control everything, I now surrender to Source and know that my abundance, my TRUE abundance, is available to me when I let go and let the Universe do the work, and I deeply and completely love and accept myself.

EARTH:

Gate 48: Wisdom

Make a list of all of your trainings, all of the skills you have, and all of the knowledge you've gleaned from your life experiences. Take some time to truly acknowledge what you know.

APRIL 1, 2024—APRIL 25, 2024
MERCURY RETROGRADE

Gate 3: The Gate of Innovation

Gate 42: The Gate of Conclusion

Gate 51: The Gate of Initiation

Retrograde cycles encourage us to go inward to explore the themes the planets give us. Mercury is the planet associated with communication. When Mercury goes retrograde it gives us an opportunity to go inward and contemplate how we can better align ourselves to have greater influence and impact in the world. Take your time to find the right words during this cycle. Do your best to not make big decisions, sign contracts, or make large purchases. Expect delays. Breathe and be patient with others.

This Mercury retrograde cycle is in powerful alignment with the big themes that have been playing out in the cosmic weather all year. We are going inward and exploring what may be blocking our path forward. As we push towards innovation and expansion, we ask ourselves: What are we grateful for? What IS working in our life? What needs to be healed, released, aligned, or finished up in order for us to awaken and connect with our higher purpose in life?

This is a powerful time to contemplate (not ACT) on what needs to be let go of to make more room. If you need to have difficult conversations at this time, wait until Mercury goes direct again. This helps you avoid reacting and misunderstanding. A great time to clean out your closets, sort through your files and do some cosmic and literal spring cleaning.

As we turn around and go direct, we'll be more deeply connected to Source, our life and soul purpose, and be prepared to harness a more powerful and deeply aligned state.

CHALLENGE:

This energy has the potential to be edgy and even shocking. Practice listening and taking this under advisement. You can always come back and address challenges in your relationships when you feel ready. It's easy to lose yourself in the name of pleasing others. Don't compromise on your true purpose and your authentic self-expression.

OPTIMAL EXPRESSION:

To use this energy to strengthen and deepen your connection to Source and your soul purpose. From this place of alignment, trust the process, take aligned action, and set the stage for growth and expansion.

UNBALANCED EXPRESSION:

To react to the feeling of lack of momentum. To push ahead and against right timing. To let frustration, anger, disappointment, and bitterness keep you stuck in a story that no longer serves you. To try to go back to how things used to be and resist the future.

CONTEMPLATIONS:

What am I grateful for? What IS working in my life? How can I create more room for growth?

What circumstances, situations, habits, and patterns need to be brought to a conclusion to make room for something new and better?

What commitment do I need to make to finish up old business?

How can I strengthen my connection to Source?

Am I living in alignment with my purpose? If not, what needs to change? What do I need to add to my life right now?

AFFIRMATION:

I am prepared for momentum. I have set the stage for my growth and expansion. By taking bold steps and actions that are in alignment with my purpose, I intentionally demonstrate to the Universe that I am ready to fulfill what I was born for. I take time and move forward with gratitude, intentionality, and in alignment with my authentic self.

APRIL 4, 2024
GATE 51: INITIATION

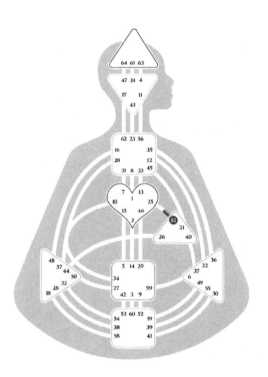

CHALLENGE:

To not let the unexpected cause you to lose your faith. To not let a pattern of unexpected events cause you to lose your connection with your purpose and Source. To learn to use the power of your own story of initiation to inspire others into fulfilling their rightful place in the cosmic plan.

JOURNAL QUESTIONS:

What has shock and the unexpected taught me in my life?

How can I deepen my connection to Source?

How can my experiences of initiation be shared with others? What am I here to wake people up to?

AFFIRMATION:

I navigate change and transformation with grace. I know that when my life takes a twist or a turn, it is my soul calling me out to serve at a higher level. I use disruption as a catalyst for my own growth and expansion. I am a teacher and an initiator. I use my ability to transform pain into growth and power to help others navigate through crisis and emerge on the other side of crisis empowered and aligned.

EFT SETUP:

Even though things are not turning out like I expected, I now choose to embrace the unexpected and trust that the Universe is always serving my greater good, and I deeply and completely love and accept myself.

EARTH:

Gate 57: Instinct

Notice your intuition this week. What does intuition feel like to you? Sometimes doing a retrospective analysis of your intuition/instinct makes it more clear about how your intuitive signals work.

APRIL 8, 2024
NEW MOON/SOLAR ECLIPSE

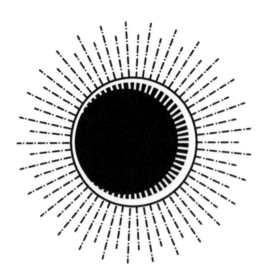

Aries 19 degrees, 23 minutes
Gate 51: The Gate of Initiation

New Moon energy invites us to explore how we can deepen our alignment with our intentions and asks us to focus on what we want to grow and expand on in our lives. Eclipse energy amplifies the intensity of the new Moon.

A Solar eclipse signifies new beginnings. Not only this, but the Solar eclipse exposes all that is hidden and not visible. The eclipse also marks an end to what has already ended. Thus, during this eclipse, many of you who did not get closure from events of the past will eventually find total closure.

This new Moon/Solar eclipse continues to highlight the cosmic dance between dismantling the old and building the new that we've been doing all year. If you've had any resistance or hesitancy in letting go and starting anew, this eclipse promises to push you and, potentially, move the rug out from under your feet so that you have no other option but to do what you may have known needed to be done a while ago.

Intuition is high at this time, but so is the fear of the future. Remember, you can't build on top of the rubble from the past. You must sweep and clear your foundation if what you're wanting to build something that is going to last. This is a powerful time to take a cosmic flashlight to the back of your dark closets and make sure there isn't any unfinished business or hidden themes that need to be brought to light so that you can make room for progress.

In the shadow, this energy can be swift and harsh. Our world may feel rocked, and we can react with shock. While there is never a guarantee that life will be easy, we certainly hedge the bets in our favor when we don't procrastinate what we know is right or inevitable. When we consciously tend to our growth and the fulfillment of our purpose, we can sometimes avoid the shocking disruptions that catalyze our growth. The Universe is gently reminding us to clean up our messes or it will do it for us.

CHALLENGE:

To not let the unexpected cause you to lose your faith. To not let a pattern of unexpected events cause you to lose your connection with your purpose and Source. To learn to use the power of your own story of initiation to initiate others into fulfilling their right place in the cosmic plan.

OPTIMAL EXPRESSION:

The ability to consciously use cycles of disruption and unexpected twists and turns of faith as catalysts that deepen your connection to Source and to your life and soul purpose.

UNBALANCED EXPRESSION:

To let the shock of disruption cause you to lose connection with your true purpose and with Source. To become bitter or angry with God. To try to control circumstance you have no control over. To become depleted from holding back your authentic self-expression.

CONTEMPLATIONS:

What has shock and the unexpected taught me in my life?

How can I deepen my connection to Source?

How can my experiences of initiation be shared with others?

What am I here to wake people up to?

AFFIRMATION:

I navigate change and transformation with grace. I know that when my life takes a twist or a turn, it is my soul calling me out to serve at a higher level. I use disruption as a catalyst for my own growth and expansion. I am a teacher and an initiator. I use my ability to transform pain into growth and power to help others navigate through crisis and emerge on the other side of the crisis, both empowered and aligned.

APRIL 10, 2024
GATE 42: CONCLUSION

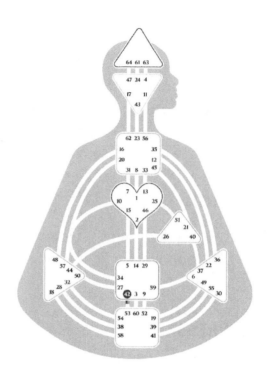

CHALLENGE:

To learn to bring things to completion. To allow yourself to be led to where you need to be to finish things. To value your ability to know how to finish and to learn to give up your need to try to start everything. To finish things in order to create space for something new.

JOURNAL QUESTIONS:

Do I own and value my natural gift of knowing how to bring things to completion?

What things in my life do I need to finish in order to make room for something new?

Am I holding on to old circumstances and patterns because I'm afraid to let them go?

Do I judge myself for not starting things? How can I learn to be gentler with myself?

AFFIRMATION:

I am gifted at knowing when and how to finish things. I respond to bringing events, experiences, and relationships to a conclusion in order to create space for something new and more abundant. I can untangle the cosmic patterns that keep people stuck in old patterns. My ability to realign and complete things helps others create space for transformation and expansion.

EFT SETUP:

Even though I have hesitated in the past to finish what I needed to be completed in order to make room for something new and better, I now choose to bring things to a powerful ending. I know that I am taking strong action to create space for what I truly want to create in my life, and I deeply and completely love myself.

EARTH:

Gate 32: Endurance

What actionable steps do you need to complete in order to be ready for creating what you want? Do one thing to lay the foundation for your dreams this week.

APRIL 16, 2024
GATE 3: INNOVATION

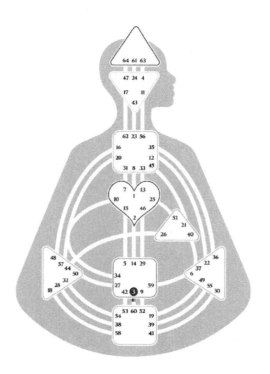

CHALLENGE:

To learn to trust in Divine timing and to know that your ideas and insights will be transmitted to the world when the world is ready.

JOURNAL QUESTIONS:

Where has Divine timing worked out in my life? What has waiting taught me?

Do I trust in Divine timing?

If the opportunity to share my ideas with the world presented itself today, would I be ready? If not, what do I need to prepare?

AFFIRMATION:

I am here to bring change to the world. My natural ability to see what else is possible to create something new is my strength and my gift. I patiently cultivate my inspiration and use my understanding of what is needed to help evolve the world.

EFT SETUP:

Even though it is scary to take the first step, I now trust the Universe and my ability to be innovative and know that I stand on the cusp of the fulfillment of my big dreams. I deeply and completely love and accept myself.

EARTH:

Gate 50: Nurturing

This week, practice taking care of yourself first—without guilt—so that you can better take care of others!

APRIL 22, 2024
GATE 27: ACCOUNTABILITY

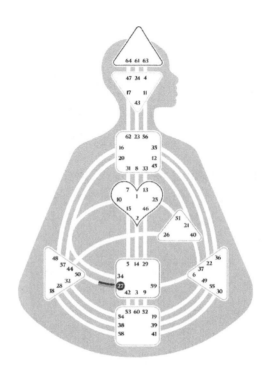

 CHALLENGE:

To care without over-caring. To allow others to assume responsibility for their own challenges and choices. To learn to accept other people's values. To not let guilt cause you to compromise what is good and right for you.

 JOURNAL QUESTIONS:

Am I taking responsibility for things that aren't mine? Whose problems are they? Can I return the responsibility for the problems back to their rightful owner?

What role does guilt play in motivating me? Can I let go of the guilt? What different choices might I make if I didn't feel guilty?

What obligations do I need to set down in order for me to take better care of myself?

Are there places where I need to soften my judgments of other people's values?

AFFIRMATION:

I have a nurturing and loving nature. It is my gift to be able to love and care for others. I know that the greatest expression of my love is to treat others as capable and powerful. I support when necessary, and I let go with love so my loved ones can discover their own strength and power.

EFT SETUP:

Even though it is hard to say no, I now choose to take the actions that are correct for me. I release my guilt, and I deeply and completely love and accept myself.

EARTH:

Gate 28: Adventure/Challenge

Where do you need to cultivate a sense of adventure in your life? Do one adventurous thing this week!

APRIL 23, 2024
FULL MOON

♏ Scorpio 4 degrees, 17 minutes
Gate 28: The Gate of Adventure/Challenge

Full Moon energy invites us to explore what we need to release and let go of in order to stay in alignment with our intentions.

We continue the very delicate dance of letting go and beginning again with this full Moon theme. We are contemplating our responsibilities and obligations and evaluating which ones are worth working towards and fighting for and which ones we need to release. Are we settling for less than what we truly want because we're trying to keep others happy? If so, it's time to unburden ourselves from this impossible task and follow the power of our dreams.

The energy of Gate 28 can be riddled with fear. Will what we're building towards be too hard? Will it be worth the effort? We're knee-deep in unknown waters and many of us may be feeling exhausted and worn out from all the changes and shifts we've already made this year. Remember, the theme this year is to draw your energy from alignment, not willpower. That means we must continue to hold a vision of what we dream of creating and trust that when the timing is right, the next right step will reveal itself. The challenge is holding the vision and taking the next right step and not getting lost in the overwhelm of the work ahead.

Gate 28 is an energy that brings drive. If your dreams are big enough and juicy enough, you'll find the energy to move forward. If you've compromised on your dreams and pared them down to make them feasible, chances are you're probably not doing what needs to be done to move the dream forward. This Moon reminds us to dream big and to not water down our dreams simply because we don't know how to make them happen.

In the shadow, this energy can be a theme that brings fighting and struggle. Remember that the only person holding you back is yourself. You owe it to yourself to recommit to your dreams and keep moving forward. Remember to prune anything—including old thoughts and beliefs—that might be holding you back from going for what you really want.

CHALLENGE:

To not let struggle and challenge leave you feeling defeated and despairing. To learn to face life as an adventure. To not let challenge and struggle cause you to feel as if you've failed.

OPTIMAL EXPRESSION:

To learn to share from your personal experience, your struggles, and your triumphs. To persevere and to know that the adventures in your life deepen your ability to transform life into a meaningful journey. To understand that your struggles help deepen the collective ideas about what is truly valuable and worthy of creating.

UNBALANCED EXPRESSION:

Refusing to take action out of fear that the journey will be too painful, wrought with struggle or lead to failure. To feel like a failure. To fall into victim consciousness.

CONTEMPLATIONS:

How can I turn my challenge into adventure?

Where do I need to cultivate a sense of adventure in my life?

What do I need to do to rewrite the story of my failures?

What meanings, blessings, and lessons have I learned from my challenges?

What needs to be healed, released, aligned, and brought to my awareness for me to trust myself and my choices?

What do I need to do to forgive myself for my perceived past failures?

AFFIRMATION:

I am here to push the boundaries of life and what is possible. I thrive in situations that challenge me. I am an explorer on the leading edge of consciousness and my job is to test how far I can go. I embrace challenges. I am an adventurer. I share all that I have learned from my challenges with the world. My stories help give people greater meaning; they teach that the world is truly worthy of creating and inspire people to transform.

APRIL 27, 2024
GATE 24: BLESSINGS

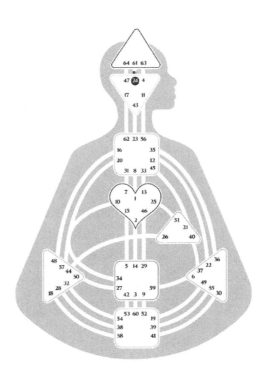

CHALLENGE:

To learn to allow what you truly deserve in your life. To not rationalize an experience that allowed for less than you deserve. To find the blessings and power from painful experiences and to use them as catalysts for transformation.

JOURNAL QUESTIONS:

What are the blessings I learned from my greatest painful experiences? Can I see how these experiences served to teach me? What did I learn?

What am I grateful for from the past?

Where might I be rationalizing staying stuck or settling for less than what I really want or deserve? What do I need to do to break out of this pattern?

AFFIRMATION:

I embrace the Mystery of Life with the awareness that the infinite generosity of the Universe gives me blessings in every event in my life. I find the blessings from the pain. I grow and expand beyond the limitations of my experiences and stories. I use what I have learned to create a life and circumstances that reflect the miracle that I am.

EFT SETUP:

Even though it is scary to start something new and I am afraid I am not ready, I now choose to courageously embrace the new and trust that everything is in Divine order, and I deeply and completely love and accept myself.

EARTH:

Gate 44: Truth

What patterns from the past are holding you back from allowing yourself to see and embody your true worth? What old patterns do you need to release this week?

MAY 3, 2024
GATE 2: ALLOWING

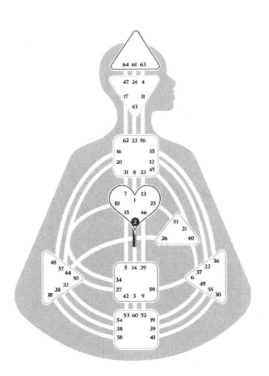

CHALLENGE:

To love yourself enough to open to the flow of support, love, and abundance. To incrementally increase over the course of your life what you're willing to allow yourself to receive. To learn to know that you are valuable and lovable simply because you exist.

JOURNAL QUESTIONS:

Do I ask for help when I need it? Why or why not?

Do I trust the Universe/God/Spirit/Source to support me in fulfilling my intentions?

Am I grateful for what I have? Make a list of everything I'm grateful for.

Can I transform my worry into trust?

Do I believe that I deserve to be supported?

AFFIRMATION:

I allow myself to receive the full flow of resources and abundance I need to fully express all of who I am. I recognize that my life is a vital, irreplaceable part of the cosmic tapestry, and I receive all that I need because it helps me contribute all that I am.

EFT SETUP:

Even though I am scared because nothing looks like I thought it would, I now choose to relax, trust, and receive the support that I am designed to receive. I know I will be supported in expressing my true self, and I deeply and completely love and accept myself.

EARTH:

Gate 1: Purpose

Spend time this week thinking about your purpose and the gifts you long to give the world. How aligned are you with your purpose?

MAY 8, 2024

NEW MOON

 Taurus 18 degrees, 1 minutes

Gate 2: The Gate of Allowing

New Moon energy invites us to explore how we can deepen our alignment with our intentions and asks us to focus on what we want to grow and expand on in our lives.

This new Moon highlights a big theme that we're focusing on in various ways for the entire year. We are healing the karma of our self-worth and bringing ourselves into alignment with our true value. This healing journey involves having very honest conversations with ourselves about how much we deserve and looking carefully at where we may have compromised or settled for less than what we truly want.

Gate 2 reminds us we're designed to be fully supported in the authentic expression of who we truly are. We are encouraged to be relentlessly authentic and to open ourselves to receive exactly what we need to fully express our unique, vital, and irreplaceable role in the cosmic plan.

This new Moon wants to explore whether you've been settling for less, or rationalizing what you want or need. Are you allowing for the support you deserve? Are you setting your standards high enough? Do you have any old stories or narratives that need to be rewritten to make room to allow for more than you have in the past? How much good are you willing to allow? Can you make room for even more?

The more you value yourself, the more the Universe sends your way.

CHALLENGE:

To love yourself enough to open to the flow of support, love, and abundance. To incrementally increase what you're willing to allow yourself to receive over the course of your life. To learn to know that you are valuable and lovable simply because you exist.

OPTIMAL EXPRESSION:

To set intentions and move solidly towards the fulfillment of the authentic self with complete trust that you are supported in being the full expression of who you are and your life purpose, even if you don't know how or what the support will look like. To trust in Source. To live in a state of gratitude.

UNBALANCED EXPRESSION:

To experience stress, fear, and ultimately compromise on what you want and who you are because you don't trust that you are supported. To be valiantly self-sufficient to the point of burning yourself out. To never ask for help.

CONTEMPLATIONS:

Do I ask for help when you need it? Why or why not?

Do I trust the Universe/God/Spirit/Source to support me in fulfilling my intentions?

Am I grateful for what I have? Make a list of everything I'm grateful for.

Can I transform my worry into trust?

Do I believe I deserve to be supported?

AFFIRMATION:

I allow myself to receive the entire flow of resources and abundance I need to express all of who I am entirely. I recognize that my life is a vital, irreplaceable part of the cosmic tapestry, and I receive all that I need because it helps me contribute to all that I am.

MAY 9, 2024
GATE 23: TRANSMISSION

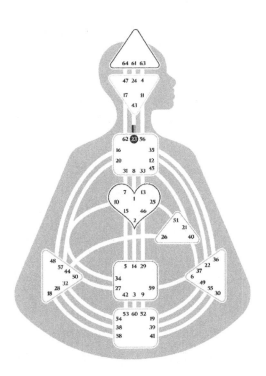

CHALLENGE:

To recognize that change and transformation are inevitable. To know what needs to happen next, to wait for the right timing and the right people to share your insights with. To not jump the gun and try to convince people to understand what you know. To not let yourself slip into negativity and despair when people aren't ready.

JOURNAL QUESTIONS:

How can I strengthen my connection to Source?

Do I trust what I know? What comes up for me when I know something, but I don't know how I know what I know?

How do I handle myself when I know something but the people around me aren't ready to hear it yet?

AFFIRMATION:

I change the world with what I know. My insights and awarenesses have the ability to transform the way people think and perceive the world. I know that my words are powerful and transformative. I trust that the people who are ready for the changes that I bring will ask me for what I know. I am a vessel for my knowingness, and I nurture myself while I wait to share what it.

EFT SETUP:

Even though in the past I shut down my voice, I now speak my truth and offer the contribution of my unique spirit to the world, and I deeply and completely love and accept myself.

EARTH:

Gate 43: Insight

This week you're learning to trust your knowingness. Practice trusting your inner knowing and the thoughts and ideas you have. Watch for self-doubt and don't discount what you know even if you don't know how you know what you know.

MAY 15, 2024
GATE 8: FULFILLMENT

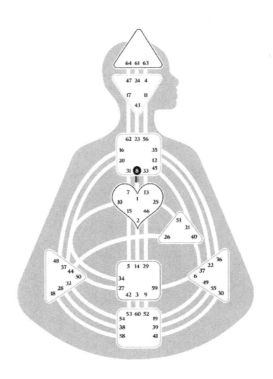

CHALLENGE:

To learn to express yourself authentically. To wait for the right people to see the value of who you are and to share yourself with them, with vulnerability and through all of your heart. To learn to trust that you are a unique expression of the Divine with a purpose and a path. To find that path and to walk it without self-judgment or holding back.

JOURNAL QUESTIONS:

Do I feel safe being vulnerable?

What experiences have caused me to feel unsafe expressing my true self? Can I rewrite those stories?

What would an uncompromising life look like for me?

What do I need to remove from my current life to make my life more authentic?

What is one bold action I can take right now that would allow me to express who I am more authentically in the world?

What is my true passion? What do I dream of?

AFFIRMATION:

I am devoted to the full expression of who I am. I defend and protect the story of my life. I know that when I am expressing myself, without hesitation or limitation, I AM the contribution that I am here to give the world. Being myself IS my life purpose and my direction flows from my authentic alignment.

EFT SETUP:

Even though I question whether I have something of value to add to the world, I now choose to courageously follow the whispers of my soul and live a life that is a powerful expression of the truth of who I am. I speak my truth. I value my contribution. I know I am precious, and I deeply and completely love and accept myself.

EARTH:

Gate 14: Creation

Ask yourself this week, "If I didn't need the money, what work would I be doing?" How is this work showing up in your life right now?

MAY 21, 2024
GATE 20: PATIENCE

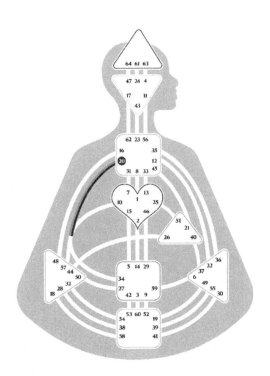

CHALLENGE:

To be patient and control the ability to wait. To be prepared and watchful but resist the urge to act if the timing isn't right or if there are details that still need to be readied.

JOURNAL QUESTIONS:

How do I manage my need for action? Am I patient?

Do I trust in Divine timing? Do I trust my intuition?

What needs to be healed, released, aligned, and brought to my awareness for me to trust my intuition?

AFFIRMATION:

I am in the flow of perfect timing. I listen to my intuition. I prepare. I gather the experience, resources, and people I need to support my ideas and my principles. When I am ready, I wait patiently, knowing that right timing is the key to transforming the world. My alignment with right timing increases my influence and my power.

EFT SETUP:

Even though it is scary to not do anything and simply wait, I now choose to trust the infinite abundance of the Universe, and I deeply and completely love and accept myself.

EARTH:

Gate 34: Power

How can you cultivate greater patience while you're waiting? What fears come up for you when you think of waiting? How can you learn to wait with patience and ease and see right timing as power?

MAY 23, 2024

FULL MOON

 Sagittarius 2 degrees, 54 minutes

Gate 34: The Gate of Power

Full Moon energy invites us to explore what we need to release and let go of in order to stay in alignment with our intentions.

The new Moon brought us an exploration in our capacity to value ourselves enough to allow the support we need and deserve into our lives. The full Moon continues with this theme, but now we're exploring the theme of power. Do we value ourselves enough to allow ourselves to fully activate our power?

Power in the Quantum Human Design chart is never about seizing, taking, or usurping. True power is energetic and vibrational. When we align with our value and our purpose, we raise our vibration and our energy field becomes attractive, compelling, and powerful. There is no need to use will to try to force someone to see things your way or to come to your perspective. You simply build a life that is worthy of emulating and your very existence draws people in and gives you a path to leadership.

Of course, because the full Moon wants us to release blocks and limitations, this Moon invites us to explore where we may be hindering our natural power, where we feel disempowered, or where we may be misusing our power because we don't trust or value ourselves enough. As has been true all year, we're simultaneously releasing and building. What old thought forms and patterns do you need to let go of in order to activate your power? Where do you need to reconnect with your power and your convictions? Where do you need to rewrite your personal narrative about your being powerful?

CHALLENGE:

To learn to measure out energy in order to stay occupied and busy but to not burn yourself out trying to force the timing or the "rightness" of a project. To wait to know which project or creation to implement based on when you get something to respond to.

OPTIMAL EXPRESSION:

The ability to respond to opportunities to unify the right people around a transformative and powerful idea when the timing and circumstances are correct.

UNBALANCED EXPRESSION:

Being too busy to tune into the right timing and the right people. Feeling frustrated with pushing and trying to make things happen. Forcing manifestation with little results. Depleting yourself because you're pushing too hard.

CONTEMPLATIONS:

Do I trust in Divine timing?

What do I need to do to deepen my trust?

How do I cultivate greater patience in my life?

What fears come up for me when I think of waiting?

How can I learn to wait with greater faith and ease?

What do I do to occupy myself while I'm waiting?

AFFIRMATION:

I am a powerful servant of Divine timing. When the timing is right, I unify the right people around the right idea and create transformation on the planet. My power is more active when I allow the Universe to set the timing. I wait. I am patient. I trust.

MAY 27, 2024
GATE 16: ZEST

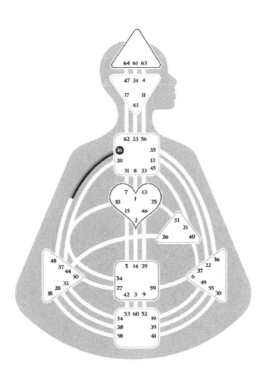

CHALLENGE:

To learn to temper your enthusiasm by making sure you are prepared enough for whatever it is you are trying to do or create.

JOURNAL QUESTIONS:

Do I trust my gut?

Do I need to slow down and make sure I've done my homework before I take action?

Have I sidelined my enthusiasm because other people have told me that I cannot do what I am dreaming of doing?

AFFIRMATION:

I am a faith-filled contagious force. I take guided actions and I trust my intuition and awareness to let me know when I am prepared and ready to leap into expanding my experience and genius. My enthusiasm inspires others to trust in themselves and to take their own giant leaps of growth.

EFT SETUP:

Even though I am afraid that I am not fulfilling my life purpose and I am wasting my life, I now choose to relax and know that I am in the perfect place at the perfect time to fulfill my destiny, and I deeply and completely love and accept myself.

EARTH:

Gate 9: Convergence

This week explore your physical environment and ask yourself if there is something in your environment that is distracting you from your focus. What can you do to improve your environment? What can you do to increase your focus?

JUNE 1, 2024
GATE 35: EXPERIENCE

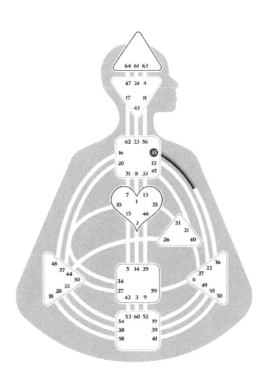

CHALLENGE:

To not let experience lead to feeling jaded or bored. To have the courage to share what you know from your experience. To know which experiences are worth participating in. To let your natural ability to become accomplished at anything keep you from being enthusiastic about learning something new. To embrace that even though you know how to know, you don't know everything.

JOURNAL QUESTIONS:

Where am I finding passion in my life? Do I need to create or discover more passion in my life right now?

Do I share my knowledge and the stories of my experiences? Do I see the value of what I have to share?

What am I curious about? How can I expand on that curiosity?

AFFIRMATION:

I am an experienced, wise, and knowledgeable resource for others. My experiences in life have added to the rich tapestry that is the story of humanity. I share my stories with others because my experiences open doorways of possibility for them. My stories help others create miracles in their lives.

EFT SETUP:

Even though in the past I struggled to stay focused and move forward, I now trust myself to take the next steps in manifesting my dream. I am focused, clear, and moving forward, and I deeply and completely love and accept myself.

EARTH:

Gate 5: Consistency

Do something symbolic this week that represents order and establishes order in your life. Clean a closet, sort through your purse or wallet. This is a good week to take stock of your habits and explore what habits might need a little refreshing or tweaking.

JUNE 6, 2024
NEW MOON

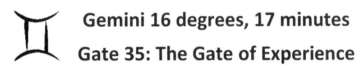

Gemini 16 degrees, 17 minutes

Gate 35: The Gate of Experience

New Moon energy invites us to explore how we can deepen our alignment with our intentions and asks us to focus on what we want to grow and expand on in our lives.

Everything about this Moon screams patience and a call to value time and timing. You can't cultivate experience and, consequently, wisdom without time, practice, and self-reflection. This new Moon invites you to make an honest assessment of your skills, your knowledge, and how your life experiences have cultivated your wisdom. What aspects of your wisdom do you need to share?

Hand in hand with this new Moon energy, we're being invited to build a practice that supports the development of our experience. We're not just taking stock of our experiences, we're building resiliency by using our experience to strengthen the skills we know we will need for the future. This new Moon invites you to ask yourself what habits and practices you need to strengthen in order to bolster your resiliency. Are you nurturing your mind, body, and spirit in such a way as to be able to integrate what you know and what you have to share?

We're also invited to release our attachment to time and timing. Everything will reveal itself in due time. Now is a good time to look back and remember all the times when things worked out and to reflect on the importance of trusting the process.

In the shadow, we discount our wisdom and experience and get seduced by the next new thing. Remember that consistency and time build wisdom and expansion. Short term solutions are, by definition, unsustainable. Build your vision towards a dream that is sustainable and enduring.

CHALLENGE:

To not let experience lead to feeling jaded or bored. To have the courage to share what you know from your experience. To know which experiences are worth participating in. To let your natural ability to become proficient at anything keep you from being enthusiastic about learning something new. To embrace that even though you know how to know, you don't know everything.

OPTIMAL EXPRESSION:

The ability to know which experiences are worthy and worthwhile. To partake in the right experience and to share your knowledge from the experience for the sake of changing the story of what's possible in the world.

UNBALANCED EXPRESSION:

To be bored with life. To let the boredom of life cause you to settle for a life that never challenges the status quo.

CONTEMPLATIONS:

Where am I finding passion in my life?

Do I need to create or discover more passion in my life right now?

Do I share my knowledge and the stories of my experiences?

Do I see the value of what I must share?

What am I curious about?

How can I expand on that curiosity?

AFFIRMATION:

I am an experienced, wise, and knowledgeable resource for others. My experiences in life have added to the rich tapestry that is the story of humanity. I share my stories with others because my experiences open doorways of possibility for others. My stories help others create miracles in their lives.

JUNE 7, 2024
GATE 45: DISTRIBUTION

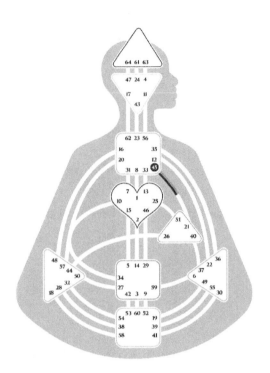

CHALLENGE:

To share and use your resources for the greater good of the whole. To learn to manage resources judiciously so that they benefit the greatest number of people. To teach as a pathway of sharing.

JOURNAL QUESTIONS:

Do I like to share? What do I have to give the world?

How do I own my right leadership? Am I comfortable as a leader?

Do I shrink from leadership? Do I overcompensate by pushing too hard with my leadership?

Do I trust that when the right people are ready, I will be pressed into action as a leader and a teacher?

What do I need to heal, release, align, or bring to my awareness to trust my leadership energy more?

AFFIRMATION:

I am a teacher and a leader. I use my resources, my knowledge, and my experience to expand the resources, knowledge, and experiences of others. I use my blessings of abundance to increase the blessings of others. I know I am a vehicle of wisdom and knowledge. I sense when it is right for me to share who I am and what I know with others.

EFT SETUP:

Even though I'm afraid to look at my finances, I now choose to take a real look at my financial numbers and know that awareness is the first step to increasing my financial status, and I deeply and completely love and accept myself.

EARTH:

Gate 26: Integrity

Where might you be experiencing a breech in your moral identity, physical resource, or energetic integrity? What do you need to do to bring yourself back into integrity?

JUNE 13, 2024
GATE 12: THE CHANNEL

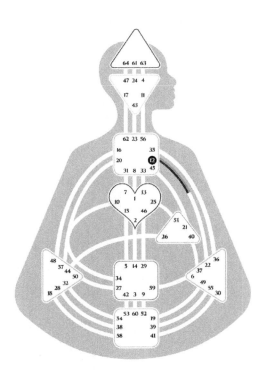

CHALLENGE:

To honor the self enough to wait for the right time and mood to speak. To know that shyness is actually a signal that the timing is not right to share transformational insights and expressions. When the timing is right, to have the courage to share what you feel and sense. To honor the fact that your voice and the words you offer are a direct connection to Source and you channel the potential for transformation. To own your creative power.

JOURNAL QUESTIONS:

How has shyness caused me to judge myself?

What do I need to do to cultivate a deeper connection with Source?

What do I need to do to connect more deeply with my creative power?

AFFIRMATION:

I am a creative being. My words, my self-expression, my creative offerings have the power to change the way people see and understand the world. I am a vessel of Divine transformation and I serve Source through the words I share. I wait for the right timing, and when I am aligned with timing and flow, my creativity creates beauty and grace in the world. I am a Divine channel, and I trust that the words I serve will open the hearts of others.

EFT SETUP:

Even though I am afraid that I am failing my life purpose and mission, I now choose to know that I am in the right place fulfilling my right purpose. All I need to do is to follow my strategy, be deliberate, follow my heart, and all will be exactly as it needs to be, and I deeply and completely love and accept myself.

EARTH:

Gate 11: The Conceptualist

Get a blank notebook and train yourself to get into the habit of writing down all of your ideas. Nurture these ideas. Dream about them. Fantasize about them and see what shows up in your life in response.

JUNE 19, 2024
GATE 15: COMPASSION

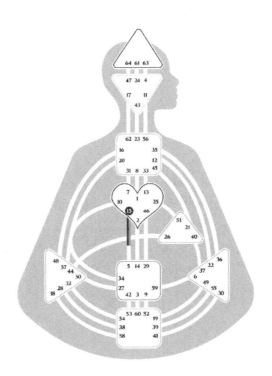

CHALLENGE:

To learn to allow yourself to be in the flow of your own rhythm. To not beat yourself up because you don't have daily habits. To have the courage to do the right thing even if you are worried about not having enough. To share from the heart without giving up your heart and serving as a martyr.

JOURNAL QUESTIONS:

Do I trust my own rhythm?

Do I share from the heart?

Do I over share?

Does my sharing compromise my own heart?

Do I judge my own rhythm?

Can I find peace in aligning with my own rhythm?

What old patterns do I need to break?

AFFIRMATION:

Like the power of a hurricane to transform the shoreline, my unique rhythm brings change to the landscape of my life and the world around me. I embrace my own rhythm and acknowledge the power of my own heart. I share with ease, and I serve my heart as the foundation of all I have to give the world.

EFT SETUP:

Even though I feel powerless to make a difference in the world, I now choose to follow my heart and my passion knowing that I am the greatest gift I can give the world. The more I show up as my true self, the more I empower others to do the same, and I deeply and completely love and accept myself.

EARTH:

Gate 10: Self-Love

This week, focus on nurturing yourself. What can you do to express love and appreciation for yourself?

JUNE 22, 2024
FULL MOON

♑ Capricorn 1 degrees, 6 minutes
Gate 10: The Gate of Self-Love

Full Moon energy invites us to explore what we need to release and let go of in order to stay in alignment with our intentions.

There is a distinct line between humility and swagger. There is also a distinct line between humility and martyrdom. True humility is knowing your right space and your right place in the world. Any less or more than that, results in a breach in integrity dooming us to spend our energy trying to prove our value.

This full Moon invites us to explore how much we not only value ourselves, but also love ourselves. While these two energies seem quite similar, self-love adds a dose of measured self-compassion and self-kindness to how we treat and see ourselves.

The root of compassion is self-love. You must love yourself in order to love at your highest level. Love without self-love leaves us vulnerable to narcissism, hidden agendas, or patterns of martyring ourselves to others. None of these ways of creating are sustainable.

Self-love is a major component of sustainability. When we love ourselves, we are better able to hold boundaries and make commitments that we can joyfully sustain. Self-love allows us to give to others without drawing from our own reserves.

This full Moon invites us to sit in quiet contemplation and genuinely assess the quality of love we have for ourselves. Self-love is not selfish. It's an essential component to generosity and abundance. How much do you love yourself? Do you love yourself enough to take care of yourself, to allow yourself to receive and to trust that you can be fulfilled in every way? When you live this way, you have an infinite well of goodness to bring to the world.

The shadow of self-love is victimhood. The challenge is learning to love yourself enough to take responsibility for your own creations or for getting out of creations that no longer serve you.

CHALLENGE:

To learn to love yourself. To learn to take responsibility for your own creations.

OPTIMAL EXPRESSION:

To see your love for yourself as the source of your true creative power.

UNBALANCED EXPRESSION:

To question your lovability, struggle to prove your love-worthiness, give up and settle for less than what you deserve, and blame others for your circumstances and situations. Victim consciousness.

CONTEMPLATIONS:

Do I love myself?

What can I do to deepen my self-love?

Where can I find evidence of my lovability in my life right now?

What do I need to do to take responsibility for situations I hate in my life right now? What needs to change?

Where am I holding blame or victimhood in my life? How could I turn that energy around?

AFFIRMATION:

I am an individuated aspect of the Divine. I am born of love. My nature is to love and be loved. I am in the full flow of giving and receiving love. I know that the quality of love I have for myself sets the direction for what I attract into my life. I am constantly increasing the quality of love I experience and share with the world.

JUNE 25, 2024
GATE 52: PERSPECTIVE

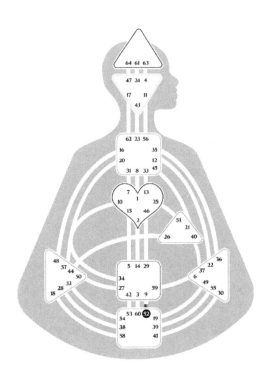

CHALLENGE:

To learn to stay focused even when you're overwhelmed by a bigger perspective. To see the big picture, to not let the massive nature of what you know confuse you and cause you to struggle with where to put your energy and attention.

JOURNAL QUESTIONS:

What do I do to maintain and sustain my focus?

Is there anything in my environment or my life that I need to move out of the way in order for me to deepen my focus?

How do I manage feeling overwhelmed?

What things am I avoiding because I feel overwhelmed by them?

What is one bold action I can take to begin clearing the path for action?

How does my feeling of being overwhelmed affect my self-worth?

How can I love myself more deeply in spite of feeling overwhelmed?

AFFIRMATION:

I am like the eagle soaring above the land. I see the entirety of what needs to happen to facilitate the evolution of the world. I use my perspective to see my unique and irreplaceable role in the cosmic plan. I see relationships and patterns that others do not always see. My perspective helps us all to build a peaceful world more effectively and in a consciously directed way.

EFT SETUP:

Even though it makes me nervous to stop doing and sit with the stillness, I now trust the process and know that my state of alignment and clarity with my intentions is the most powerful thing I can do to create effectively and powerfully in my life. I relax, I trust and let my abundance unfold, and I deeply and completely love and accept myself.

EARTH:

Gate 58: Joy

Do at least five things this week simply for the joy of it. Notice how joy feels and commit to cultivating more joy in your daily practice.

JULY 1, 2024
GATE 39: RECALIBRATION

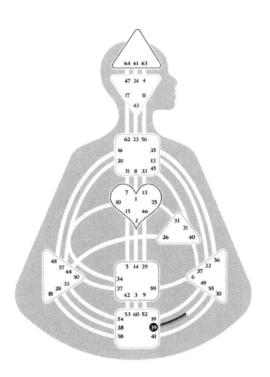

CHALLENGE:

To challenge and tease out energies that are not in alignment with faith and abundance. To bring them to awareness and to use them as pushing off points to deepen faith and trust in Source.

JOURNAL QUESTIONS:

Do I trust Source?

What do I need to do to deepen my trust in Source?

Do I feel like I am enough?

Do I feel like I have enough?

Take stock of everything I have and everything I've been given. Do I have enough? Have I ever not been supported?

What do I have that I'm grateful for?

Have I abdicated my own power to create?

What needs to be healed, released, aligned, or brought to my awareness to reactivate my power to create my own abundance?

AFFIRMATION:

I am deeply calibrated with my faith. I trust that I am fully supported. I use experiences that create desire and wanting as opportunities to deepen my faith that I will receive and create all that I need to fulfill my mind, body, and spirit. I am in the perfect flow of abundance, and I am deeply aligned with Source.

EFT SETUP:

Even though I worry about money, having the right relationship, and creating abundance in every area of my life, I now trust Spirit and allow the abundant nature of the Universe to reveal itself to me. I stay open to the possibilities of miracles and trust that all I have to do is stay conscious of the abundance of Spirit unfolding within me, and I deeply and completely love and accept myself.

EARTH:

Gate 38: The Visionary

One of the biggest things that can shut you down and cause you to procrastinate is not having a big enough dream. If you were going to blow the edges and limitations off of your dream, what would you create with your life? What is your really, really big dream? Spend some time imagining the fulfillment of your dream this week.

JULY 5, 2024

NEW MOON

 Cancer 14 degrees, 23 minutes

Gate 43: The Gate of Recalibration

New Moon energy invites us to explore how we can deepen our alignment with our intentions and asks us to focus on what we want to grow and expand on in our lives.

Gate 39 pushes us towards our abundance. This energy, in the shadow, can feel provocative and challenging. Those of us who carry this energy in our chart are often known for being a bit edgy and maybe a wee bit too honest about what's blocking the path.

The theme of this new Moon blesses us with the ability to see what's standing in the way of our abundance. We are invited with the initiation of this Moon to dig deep and explore what is keeping us from creating with faith. Allow the messages and the clarity to drop in today as you focus on what you want and hold the vision of how it will feel when your dreams come true.

There is a slight tug-of-war here with the celestial weather. We're starting to catch our breath with this new Moon after a rather bumpy year. There's an enthusiastic quest to move forward as fast as possible. But before we can run away from the past, we have to first figure out what we're running toward and make sure the path is clear for expansion. Use this new Moon energy wisely. Ask for all obstacles to be clarified and then removed so that you get maximum traction as you build forward!

Be patient with those around you. This energy can make us feel tense. Do your best to not take anything personally and wait for this tension to pass.

CHALLENGE:

To challenge and tease out energies that are not in alignment with faith and abundance. To bring them to awareness and to use them as pushing-off points to deepen faith and trust in Source.

OPTIMAL EXPRESSION:

The ability to transform an experience into an opportunity to shift toward greater abundance. To see and experience internal or external lack and to use your awareness of lack to recalibrate your energy toward sufficiency and abundance.

UNBALANCED EXPRESSION:

Feeling overwhelmed by lack and panicking. Hoarding and over-shopping as a result of fear of scarcity. Provoking and challenging others and holding others responsible for your inner alignment with sufficiency.

CONTEMPLATIONS:

Do I trust Source?

What do I need to do to deepen my trust in Source?

Do I feel like I am enough?

Do I feel like I have enough?

Take stock of everything I have and everything I have been given.

Do I have enough?

Have I ever really not been supported?

What do I have that I'm grateful for?

Have I abdicated my own power to create?

What needs to be healed, released, aligned, or brought to my awareness to reactivate my power to create my own abundance?

AFFIRMATION:

I am deeply calibrated with my faith. I trust that I am fully supported. I use experiences that create desire and wanting in me as opportunities to deepen my faith that I will receive and create all I need to fulfill my mind, body, and Spirit. I am in the perfect flow of abundance, and I am deeply aligned with Source.

JULY 7, 2024
GATE 53: STARTING

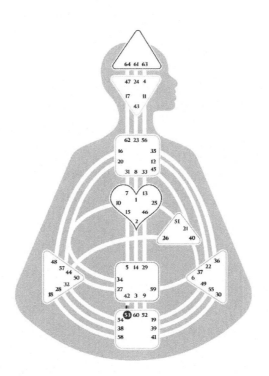

CHALLENGE:

To respond in alignment with your energy blueprint to opportunities to get things started. To initiate the process of preparing or "setting the state" for the manifestation of a dream before it becomes a reality. To learn to trust in the timing of the Universe and not take charge and try to implement your own ideas while working against Divine timing. To not burn out trying to complete things. To find peace as a "starter," not a "finisher."

JOURNAL QUESTIONS:

How do I feel about myself when I have an idea and I can't get it initiated?

How do I feel when someone takes my initial idea and builds on it?

Do I value what I started?

What identities and attachments do I have to being the one who starts and finishes something?

Do I judge myself for not finishing something?

How can I be gentler with myself?

Do I trust Divine timing?

How can I deepen my trust in right timing?

AFFIRMATION:

I am a servant to Divine Inspiration. My thoughts, inspirations, and ideas set the stage for creative expansion and the potential for evolution. I take action on the ideas that present themselves to me in an aligned way. I honor all other ideas knowing that my gift is in the spark of energy that gets things rolling when the timing is right. While I wait for right timing, I guard my energy and charge my battery so that I am sustainable when the time is right for action.

EFT SETUP:

Even though I am scared to believe that my big dreams could come true, I now choose to trust the infinite power of the Universe and know that I am never given a dream that can't be fulfilled, and I deeply and completely love and accept myself.

EARTH:

Gate 54: Divine Inspiration

Is there anything you need to do or prepare to be ready for the next step in manifesting your dream or inspiration?

JULY 13, 2024
GATE 62: PREPARATION

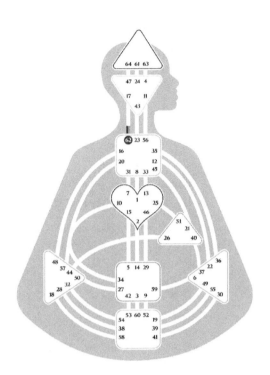

CHALLENGE:

To trust that you will be prepared for the next step. To not let worry and over-preparation distract you from being present in the moment. To let the fear of not being ready keep you trapped.

JOURNAL QUESTIONS:

Do I worry? What do I do to manage my worry?

What can I do to trust that I know what I need to know?

What proof do I have that I am in the flow of preparation?

Is there anything in my life right now that I need to plan for?

Am I over-planning? Does my need for contingency plans keep me stuck?

AFFIRMATION:

I create the foundation for the practice of excellence by engineering the plan of action that creates growth. I am in the flow of my understanding, and I use my knowledge and experience to be prepared for the evolution of what is next. I am ready and I am prepared. I trust my own preparation and allow myself to be in the flow of what is next knowing that I will know what I need to know when I need to know it.

EFT SETUP:

Even though I feel pressure to do something, I now choose to relax and trust the power of my dreams to call the right circumstance to me, and I deeply and completely love and accept myself.

EARTH:

Gate 61: Wonder

This week, take some time to look up at the sky. Go somewhere, if possible, where you can see the stars and gaze at the face of the Cosmos with awe. Bring the feeling of awe into your everyday life.

JULY 19, 2024
GATE 56: EXPANSION

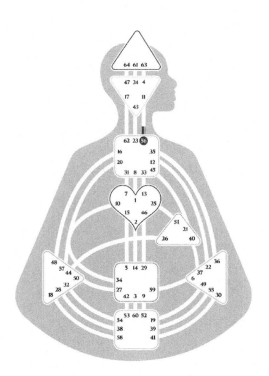

CHALLENGE:

To learn to share stories and inspirations with the right people at the right time. To learn to tell stories of expansion and not depletion and contraction.

JOURNAL QUESTIONS:

What stories do I share repeatedly with others?

Do they lift people up or cause them to contract?

What stories do I tell about myself and my voice that cause me to either expand or contract?

What am I here to inspire others to do or be?

AFFIRMATION:

I am a Divine storyteller. The stories of possibility that I share have the power to inspire others to grow and expand. I use my words as a template for possibility and expansion for the world. I inspire the world with my words.

EFT SETUP:

Even though I'm afraid to share my ideas, I now choose to take leadership with my inspirations and share my precious ideas with others, and I deeply and completely love and accept myself.

EARTH:

Gate 60: Conservation

Gratitude is the gateway to transformation. This week, take stock of everything in your life that is good and that is working. Make a daily list of the things you're grateful for.

JULY 21, 2024
FULL MOON

 Capricorn 29 degrees, 8 minutes

Gate 60: The Gate of Conservation

Full Moon energy invites us to explore what we need to release and let go of in order to stay in alignment with our intentions.

Growth always follows cycles of disruption and upheaval. All the changes and transformations we've experienced this year have been symptoms of us outgrowing our old stories and narratives. When we go through these big cycles of change, we are always forced to confront how we choose to move forward. We can resist and try to go back to how things used to be, but that is never a true option. The person you were before is gone and they are never coming back.

The second option is to take stock of what is working in your life and focus on that. When we are grateful for the things in our life that we want to expand upon, we ultimately cultivate the ability to innovate. Gratitude is the currency of growth. This full Moon gives us a shining invitation to take stock of what is good in your life and spend some time being grateful. This shift in perspective not only activates a state of heart coherence and enhances creativity, but it also literally creates higher states of physical well-being and programs the brain to notice opportunities to see more of the good stuff!

What are you grateful for? What is good in your life? How can you express your gratitude for all that is well in your life?

CHALLENGE:

To not let the fear of loss overwhelm your resourcefulness. To learn to find what is working and focus on it instead of looking at the loss and disruption.

OPTIMAL EXPRESSION:

The ability to find the blessings in transformation. Optimism. To know how to focus on what is working instead of what's not.

UNBALANCED EXPRESSION:

To hold on and not allow for growth. To fight for the old and rebuke change. To let the overwhelm of change and disruption create paralysis and resistance.

CONTEMPLATIONS:

What change am I resisting?

What am I afraid of?

What are the things in my life (that are working) that I need to focus on?

Is my fear of loss holding me back?

AFFIRMATION:

I am grateful for all the transformation and change in my life. I know that disrupttion is the catalyst for my growth. I am able to find the blessings of the past and incorporate them into my innovative vision for the future. I am optimistic about the future, and I transform the world by growing what works.

JULY 24, 2024
GATE 31: THE LEADER

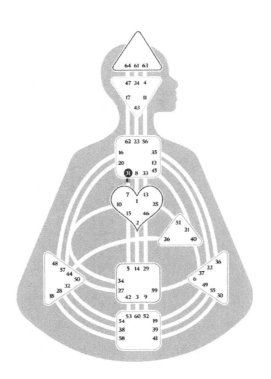

 CHALLENGE:

To learn to lead as a representative of the people you are leading. To cultivate a leadership agenda of service. To not let your fear of not being seen, heard, or accepted get in the way of healthy leadership. To learn to take your rightful place as a leader and not hide out.

 JOURNAL QUESTIONS:

How do I feel about being a leader?

Am I comfortable leading?

Do I shrink from assuming leadership?

What is my place of service? Who do I serve?

AFFIRMATION:

I am a natural born leader. I serve at my highest potential when I am empowering others by giving them a voice and then serving their needs. I use my power to lead people to a greater expansion of who they are and to support them in increasing their abundance, sustainability, and peace.

EFT SETUP:

Even though I'm afraid to be seen, I now choose to express myself and the magnificence that is me with gusto, courage, awareness of my own power and preciousness, and I deeply and completely love and accept myself.

EARTH:

Gate 41: Imagination

Your imagination is one of the most powerful creative tools you have access to. Spend time this week practicing using your imagination. What do you dream of? What other possibilities are there? Use your imagination to "see" other potential realities. You don't have to "do" what you imagine. Just use this power to stimulate creative emotional frequencies of energy.

JULY 30, 2024
GATE 33: RETELLING

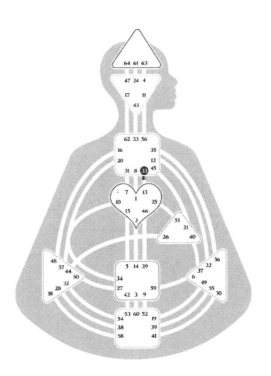

CHALLENGE:

To learn to share a personal narrative that reflects your true value and your worth. To share a personal narrative when it serves the intention to serve, improving the direction of others. To share history in an empowering way.

JOURNAL QUESTIONS:

What personal narratives am I telling that might be keeping me stuck, feeling like a victim, or feeling unlovable? How can I rewrite these stories?

What listening practices do I have? What can I do to listen better so that I can gauge the right time to share in a powerful way?

AFFIRMATION:

I am a processor of stories. My gift is my ability to help others find blessings, love, and power from stories of pain. I hold people's secrets and stories and transform them to share when the time is right. The stories I tell change the direction of people's lives. I use the power of stories to increase the power of heart in the world and to help build a world of love.

EFT SETUP:

Even though my stories from my past have held me back, I now choose to rewrite the story of my life and tell it the way I choose. I do so with forgiveness, embracing the gifts and honoring my courage and strength in my story, and I deeply and completely love and accept myself.

EARTH:

Gate 19: Attunement

This week, spend some time alone in nature. Really feel how your energy appears in the restful embrace of the natural world. Practice feeling and sensing the energy of others and then contrasting it with your own so that you can better learn to distinguish your energy from the emotional energy around you.

AUGUST 4, 2024
NEW MOON

 Leo 12 degrees, 33 minutes

Gate 33: The Gate of Re-Telling

New Moon energy invites us to explore how we can deepen our alignment with our intentions and asks us to focus on what we want to grow and expand on in our lives.

This new Moon invites us to reprogram what we seek to build in our lives by telling bigger and better stories. We have been learning all year to surrender and to allow grace to reveal to us the next right step, followed by the next one and then the next one. We've been learning to trust the process and to stay in the flow of creative expansion by learning to align with the true story of who we really are. Remember, the overarching theme of this year is to create with the spark of magic that accompanies being authentic, rather than pushing with will to override divine timing and perfect circumstances.

The stories we tell ourselves and the world about who and how we are set the tone and the direction for our lives.

This new Moon offers a sweeping opportunity to retell all the stories of your life in the way you choose. Are your stories holding the energy of victimhood? Rewrite them so that you emerge from the story empowered and blessed. Are your stories holding energies of lack? Retell them so they are abundant and expansive.

We are deeply sensitive and potentially emotionally open this week. So are the people around us.

This gives you a great opportunity to examine your relationship stories and make sure that the story you choose for yourself isn't watered down or being told in such a way that you give up what you need and want to keep others happy. Telling an empowered and abundant story never takes away from or diminishes another person.

What stories will you reclaim sovereignty over?

CHALLENGE:

To learn to share a personal narrative that reflects your true value and your worth. To share a personal narrative when it supports the intention to serve in improving the direction of others. To share history in an empowering way.

OPTIMAL EXPRESSION:

The ability to translate a personal experience into an empowering narrative that teaches and gives direction to others. Finding the power from the pain. Waiting for the right timing to transform or share a narrative so that it has the greatest impact on the heart of another.

UNBALANCED EXPRESSION:

Staying stuck and sharing a personal narrative rooted in pain, disempowerment, and victimhood.

CONTEMPLATIONS:

What personal narratives am I repeating that might be keeping me stuck, feeling like a victim, or feeling unlovable?

How can I rewrite these stories?

What listening practices do I have?

What can I do to listen better so I can gauge when it is the right time to share in a powerful way?

AFFIRMATION:

I am a processor of stories. My gift is my ability to help others find the blessings, the love, and the power from stories of pain. I hold people's secrets and stories and transform them to share when the time is right. The stories I tell change the direction of people's lives. I use the power of stories to increase the power of heart in the world and to help build a world of love.

AUGUST 5, 2024
GATE 7: COLLABORATION

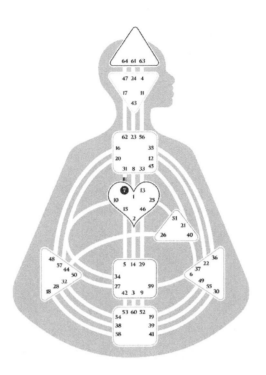

CHALLENGE:

To understand the need to be in front and allow yourself to serve through building teams, collaborating, and influencing the figurehead of leadership. To be at peace serving the leader through support and collaboration. To recognize that the voice of the leader is only as strong and powerful as the support they receive.

JOURNAL QUESTIONS:

What are my gifts and strengths? How do I use those gifts to influence and lead others?

How do I feel about not being the figurehead of leadership?

What happens when I only support the leadership? Do I still feel powerful? Influential?

Make a list of the times when my influence has positively directed leadership.

AFFIRMATION:

I am an agent of peace who influences the direction and organization of leadership. I unify people around ideas. I influence with my wisdom, my knowledge, and my connections. I am a team builder, a collaborator, and I organize people in ways that empower them and support them in creating a collective direction rooted in compassion.

EFT SETUP:

Even though I feel confused and conflicted about what to do, I trust the Divine flow and let the Universe show me the right thing to do in the right time, and I deeply and completely love, trust, and accept myself.

EARTH:

Gate 13: Narrative

Take time this week to really listen to the story you're telling about who you are. Is it big enough? Are you taking control of your own story or are you allowing the past to define who you are? If you were going to rewrite your story, what would you say about yourself? How can you make your personal narrative truer to who you really are?

AUGUST 5, 2024—AUGUST 28, 2024
MERCURY RETROGRADE

Gate 59: The Gate of Sustainability

Gate 29: The Gate of Devotion

Gate 4: The Gate of Possibility

Retrograde cycles encourage us to go inward to explore the themes that the planets give us. Mercury is the planet associated with communication. When Mercury goes retrograde, it gives us an opportunity to go inward and contemplate how we can better align ourselves to have greater influence and impact in the world. Take your time to find the right words during this cycle. Do your best to not make big decisions, sign contracts, or make large purchases. Expect delays. Breathe and be patient with others.

This Mercury retrograde, we are drawing inward and asking ourselves what we need to do to stay sustainable, avoid burnout, and find a spark of energy that can keep us moving forward after all the change and transformation this year has brought.

It's easy to think that we can use force or sheer effort to push through life, but this retrograde cycle is reminding us that pushing is finite. We can only push so far before our energy or resources fail us. We can harness a more consistent and effective quality of energy when we wait, see what shows up and, most importantly, cultivate a deep and devoted practice that anchors our mind, body, and spirit in the energy of possibility.

It's easy to be doubtful. We've been living with the idea for hundreds of years that hard work creates more. Now we're learning that we create more and experience greater creativity when we rest, trust Source, and self-regulate our energy as an essential way to see new possibilities and creative options. You absolutely CAN heal, rest, and align and simultaneously be supported and abundant.

CHALLENGE:

To learn to relax and trust the process. No amount of pushing, resisting, or forcing is going to create what you want. Energy is of a premium and we have to harness it in such a way that we stay sustainable, and we can do the work that produces enduring results and resources.

OPTIMAL EXPRESSION:

To cultivate a devoted practice that deepens your connection to Source. To wait and see what shows up in your life and to allow the next right step to unfold instead of pushing and frantically searching for the answer. To rest and heal and allow yourself to be supported.

UNBALANCED EXPRESSION:

To frantically look for the answers and the opportunities to create what you think you need. To fail to rest and nurture yourself because you're afraid to trust. To push and force an idea born of desperation.

CONTEMPLATIONS:

What is my spiritual practice? How do I stay connected to Source?

What is my definition of success? Am I being successful right now?

Do I feel vital? Do I need to heal my energy?

What creative play do I allow in my life? How can I create more?

AFFIRMATION:

I am an integral and vital aspect of the cosmic plan. My life is so important that I am afforded the time to rest and renew myself. When I nurture myself, my capacity for creativity and expansion increases exponentially. I am fully supported, deeply loved, and magnificently powerful. All I have to do is relax, take care of myself, and trust the process.

AUGUST 11, 2024
GATE 4: POSSIBILITY

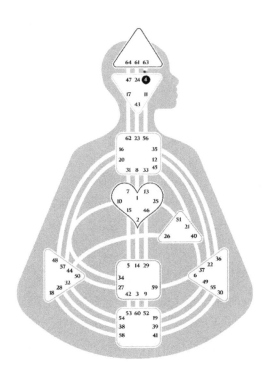

CHALLENGE:

To learn to embrace ideas as possibilities, not answers, and to let the power of the possibility stimulate the imagination as a way of calibrating the emotions and the heart. This Gate teaches us the power of learning to wait to see which possibility actually manifests in the physical world and to experiment with options in response.

JOURNAL QUESTIONS:

What ideas do I have right now that need me to nurture and activate them?

What possibilities do these ideas stimulate right now? Take some time to write or visualize the possibilities.

Am I comfortable with waiting? What can I do to increase my patience and curiosity?

AFFIRMATION:

I am tuned into the cosmic flow of possibility. I am inspired to explore new possibilities and potentials. I use the power of my thoughts to stretch the limits of what is known and engage my imagination to explore the potential of the unknown.

EFT SETUP:

Even though I don't know what to do, I allow my questions to seed the Universe and I trust and wait with great patience that the answers will be revealed to me, and I deeply and completely love and accept myself.

EARTH:

Gate 49: The Catalyst

Are you holding onto a situation for too long? Do you have a habit of quitting too soon? Is there a circumstance or condition in your life that you are allowing or running from because you fear the emotional energy associated with change? What needs to be healed or released?

AUGUST 17, 2024
GATE 29: DEVOTION

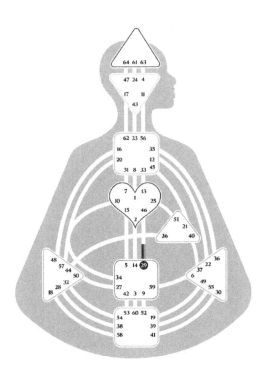

CHALLENGE:

To discover what and who you need to devote yourself to. To sustain yourself so that you can sustain so that you have the energy to keep going. To learn to say no to what you need to say no to and to learn to say yes to what you want to say yes to.

JOURNAL QUESTIONS:

What devotion do I have right now that drives me?

Is this a devotion that inspires me, or do I feel overly obligated to it?

Who would I be and what would I choose if I gave myself permission to say no more often?

What would I like to say no to that I am saying yes to right now?

What obligations do I need to take off my plate right now?

What would I like to devote myself to?

AFFIRMATION:

I have an extraordinary ability to devote myself to the manifestation of an idea. My commitment to my story and to the fulfillment of my intention changes the story of what is possible in my own life and for humanity. I choose my commitments with great care. I devote myself to what is vital for the evolution of the world, and I nurture myself first because my well-being is the foundation of what I create.

EFT SETUP:

Even though I am afraid to invest all my effort into my dream (what if it fails... what if I'm crazy... what if I just need to buckle down and be "normal" ...), I now choose to do it anyway, and I deeply and completely love and accept myself.

EARTH:

Gate 30: Passion

What do you need to do this week to sustain your vision or dream about what you are inspired to create in your life?

AUGUST 19, 2024
FULL MOON

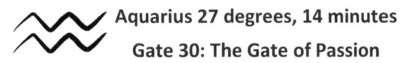 **Aquarius 27 degrees, 14 minutes**

Gate 30: The Gate of Passion

Full Moon energy invites us to explore what we need to release and let go of in order to stay in alignment with our intentions.

Passion is the fuel that keeps us moving toward creative expansion. Creating with passion brings us energy and drive to keep going, even when things feel bumpy or challenging.

We often think of passion as being a spark, a temporary flare of energy, but passion in Quantum Human Design is an energy that is designed to be cultivated and tended to. There is a difference between an eternal flame versus a conflagration. To truly cultivate the flame of passion and keep it burning requires commitment and devotion. It takes time, practice, and conscious awareness to tend to the spark of your creativity.

This full Moon invites us to explore our commitment and devotion to our passion. Are we practicing, cultivating, and honing our talents, taking time to bring the energy of consistency and repetition to the process of growth? What needs to shift in life to call in a consistent fuel for your passion?

Passion without devotion is destructive. Passion as a practice ushers in the new and has the potential to shatter old patterns and harness the power of miracles. Passion with practice brings form to imagination. Passion without practice brings the potential for burnout and lack of fulfillment.

CHALLENGE:

To sustain a dream or a vision without burning out. To know which dream to be passionate about. To not let passion overwhelm you and to wait for the right timing to share your passion with the world.

OPTIMAL EXPRESSION:

The ability to sustain a dream, intention, and a vision until you bring it into form. To inspire others with the power of your dream. To inspire passion in others.

UNBALANCED EXPRESSION:

Burnout. Impatience and not waiting for the right timing. Misdirected passion that is perceived as too much intensity. Leaping into chaos.

CONTEMPLATIONS:

What am I passionate about?

Have I lost my passion?

How is my energy?

Am I physically burned out?

Am I burned out on my idea?

What do I need to do to sustain my vision or dream about what I am inspired to create in my life?

Do I have a dream or vision I are avoiding because I am afraid it won't come true?

AFFIRMATION:

I am a passionate creator. I use the intensity of my passion to increase my emotional energy and sustain the power of my dream and what I imagine for life. I trust in the Divine flow, and I wait for the right timing and the right circumstances to act on my dream.

AUGUST 23, 2024
GATE 59: SUSTAINABILITY

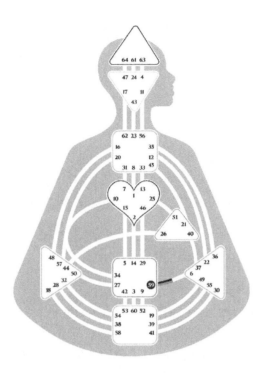

CHALLENGE:

To learn to make abundant choices that sustain you, and at the same time, others. To collaborate and initiate others into sustainable relationships from a place of sufficiency. To learn to share what you have in a sustainable way.

JOURNAL QUESTIONS:

Do I trust in my own abundance?

How do I feel about sharing what I have with others?

Am I creating relationship and partnership agreements that honor my work?

Do I have relationships and agreements that are draining me? What needs to change?

How do I feel about being right?

Am I open to other ways of thinking or being?

Do I believe in creating agreements and alignments with people who have different values and perspectives?

AFFIRMATION:

The energy I carry has the power to create sufficiency and sustainability for all. I craft valuable alliances and agreements that support me in expanding abundance for everyone. I hold to higher principles and values that are rooted in my trust in sufficiency and the all-providing Source. Through my work and alignments, my blessings serve to increase the blessings of myself and others.

EFT SETUP:

Even though I struggle to share my intentions, I now choose to boldly state them and wait for the pieces of my creation to magically fall into place, and I deeply and completely love and accept myself.

EARTH:

Gate 55: Faith

This week, deepen your experience of beauty. Surround yourself with beauty. Consciously bring beauty into your daily life and notice how abundantly beautiful life truly is.

AUGUST 29, 2024
GATE 40: RESTORATION

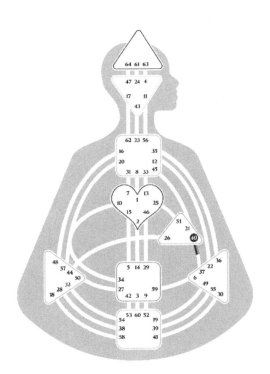

 CHALLENGE:

To learn to value yourself enough to retreat from community and the energy of those you love to restore, restock, and replenish your inner resources. To learn to interpret the signal of loneliness correctly. To take responsibility for your own care and resources and to not abdicate your power to take care of yourself.

 JOURNAL QUESTIONS:

What role does loneliness play in my life?

Has loneliness caused me to doubt my value?

What do I need to do to restore my energy?

Am I doing enough to take care of myself?

What agreements am I making in my relationships that might be causing me to compromise my value?

How can I rewrite these agreements?

Am I abdicating my responsibility for my self-care?

Am I living a martyr model?

What needs to be healed, released, aligned, and brought to my awareness for me to take responsibility for cultivating my own sense of value and my self-worth?

AFFIRMATION:

I am a powerful resource for my community. The energy that I hold impacts others deeply and brings them to deeper states of alignment and sustainability. I take care of my body, mind, and soul because I know the more that I am and the more that I have, the more I can give to others. I take care of myself first because I know that good things flow from me. I am valuable and powerful, and I claim and defend the true story of Who I Truly Am.

EFT SETUP:

Even though it is hard to let go of the obligations of relationships, I now choose to release all relationships that are draining and unsupportive, and I deeply and completely love and accept myself.

EARTH:

Gate 37: Peace

When you feel that your outer world is chaotic and disrupted, how do you cultivate inner peace? Practice anchoring yourself in deep inner peace this week.

SEPTEMBER 3, 2024
GATE 64: DIVINE TRANSFERENCE

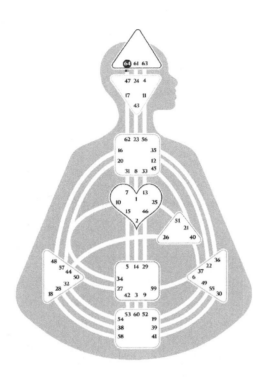

CHALLENGE:

To not let the power of your big ideas overwhelm you and shut down your dreaming and creating. To not get lost in the pressure of answering the how question.

JOURNAL QUESTIONS:

What do I do to take care of my big ideas?

How do I feel about having dreams but not always the solutions?

How can I stop judging the gift of my dreams?

Do I trust that the how of my ideas will be revealed?

How can I deepen this trust?

AFFIRMATION:

I am a conduit for expansive thinking. My inspirations and ideas create the seeds of possibility in my mind and in the mind of others. I honor the dreams that pass through my mind and allow my big ideas to stimulate my imagination and the imagination of others. I trust the Universe to reveal the details of my dreams when the time is right. I use the power of my dreams to stimulate a world of possibility and expansion.

EFT SETUP:

Even though I don't know what is next, I wait and trust that the perfect right step will show up for me, and I deeply and completely love and accept myself.

Even though I feel overwhelmed with ideas, I trust the Universe to reveal the next step to me. I relax and wait, and I deeply and completely love and accept myself.

EARTH:

Gate 63: Curiosity

What needs to happen to unlock your attachment to being right and to allow yourself to dream of other possibilities? What if there's more than what you can see right now?

SEPTEMBER 3, 2024
NEW MOON

 Virgo 21 degrees, 28 minutes

Gate 64: The Gate of Divine Transference

New Moon energy invites us to explore how we can deepen our alignment with our intentions and asks us to focus on what we want to grow and expand on in our lives.

With the outer planets all holding a retrograde station right now, it's easy to feel like we're caught in "cosmic goo." We're all revved up with big ideas and no real way to implement them. We're forced to sit with the pressure of trying to figure out how to turn our ideas into action and to practice waiting for the epiphany that will reveal the next right step.

This energy can feel heavy if we resist it but can feel dreamy and filled with possibility if we simply allow ourselves to pause and savor our inspirations. In the shadow, we doubt ourselves and grapple with confusion if we don't produce the answer to our musings on command. We succumb to the pressure and turn away from our dreams, defaulting to old ideas and our mental conditioning, leaving us feeling bitter and defeated.

The power of using this Moon energy lies in the willingness to trust that the answers to how will reveal themselves in due time. In the meantime, savor the inspirations that have been revealed to you. Be a steward for your ideas and give them lots of love, dream time, and attention!

CHALLENGE:

To not let the power of your big ideas overwhelm you and shut down dreaming and creating. To get lost in the pressure of answering the question of how.

OPTIMAL EXPRESSION:

The ability to receive a big idea and to serve the idea by giving it your imagination and dreaming. To trust that you'll know how to implement the idea if it is yours to make manifest. To hold the energy of an idea for the world.

UNBALANCED EXPRESSION:

To feel pressure to manifest a big idea. To feel despair or inadequate or ungrounded if you don't know how to make an idea a reality. To feel deep mental pressure to figure out an idea. To give up dreaming.

CONTEMPLATIONS:

What do I do to take care of my big ideas?

How do I feel about having dreams but not always the solutions?

How can I stop judging the gift of my dreams?

Do I trust that the how of my ideas will be revealed?

How can I deepen this trust?

AFFIRMATION:

I am a conduit for expansive thinking. My inspirations and ideas create the seeds of possibility in my mind and the mind of others. I honor the dreams that pass through my mind and allow my big ideas to stimulate my imagination and the imagination of others. I trust the Universe to reveal the details of my dreams when the time is right. I use the power of my dreams to stimulate a world of possibility and expansion.

SEPTEMBER 9, 2024
GATE 47: MINDSET

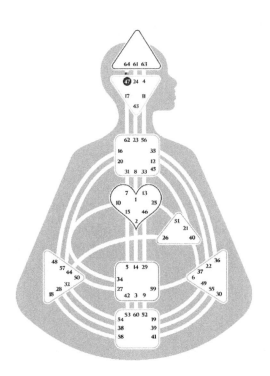

CHALLENGE:

To become skilled at a mindset of openness and possibility. To not let inspiration die because you don't know how to fulfill it.

JOURNAL QUESTIONS:

What thoughts do I have when I receive an idea or inspiration?

Am I hopeful or despairing?

How does it feel to let go of figuring out how I'm going to make my idea a reality?

What do I do to regulate my mindset?

What practices do I need to cultivate to increase the power of my thoughts?

AFFIRMATION:

My mindset is the source of my inspired actions and attitude. I know that when I receive an idea and inspiration, it is my job to nurture the idea by using the power of my imagination to increase the potential and emotional frequency of the idea. I consistently keep my inner and outer environment aligned with the energy of possibility and potential. I know it is my job to create by virtue of my alignment, and I relax knowing it is the job of the Universe to fulfill my inspirations.

EFT SETUP:

Even though it is frustrating to not know how to make something happen, I now choose to wait for Divine Insight, and I trust the right information will be revealed to me at the perfect time, and I deeply and completely love and accept myself.

EARTH:

Gate 22: Surrender

Where are you denying your passion in your life? What is one thing you can do this week to reclaim your passion?

SEPTEMBER 15, 2024
GATE 6: IMPACT

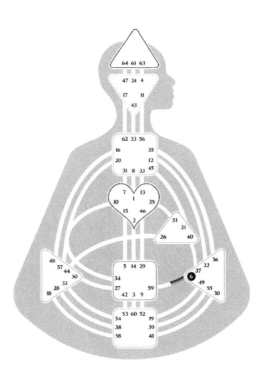

CHALLENGE:

To become proficient in using emotional energy and learn to trust that your impact is in service to the world. When you understand that your life is a vehicle for service and your energy is being used to influence and impact those around you, you assume greater obligation and responsibility to maintaining a high frequency of energy. The quality of the emotional energy you cultivate influences others to come together in an equitable, sustainable, and peaceful way. Learning to trust that your words and impact will have effect when the timing is correct and not overriding Divine timing.

JOURNAL QUESTIONS:

What do I need to do to deepen my trust in Divine timing?

How do I prepare myself to be seen and to have influence?

What do I need to do to regulate my emotional energy in order to align with peaceful and sustainable solutions?

Do I trust in the abundance of the Universe?

AFFIRMATION:

My emotional energy influences the world around me. I am rooted in the energy of equity, sustainability, and peace. When I am aligned with abundance, I am an energetic source of influence that facilitates elegant solutions to creating peace and well-being. I am deliberate and aligned with values that create peace in my life, in my community, and in the world.

EFT SETUP:

Even though I am ready to leap into action, I now choose to take a breath, wait out my emotions, and trust that the right timing will be revealed to me. I'm not missing out on anything. Divine Order is the rule of the day, and I deeply and completely love and accept myself.

EARTH:

Gate 36: Exploration

Go on a "miracle hunt" today. Make a list of all the unexpected synchronous and serendipitous events that have happened in your life. What has been the greatest miracle or unexpected event you've experienced in your life?

SEPTEMBER 18, 2024
FULL MOON/ LUNAR ECLIPSE

♓ Pisces 25 degrees, 41 minutes
Gate 36: The Gate of Exploration

Full Moon energy invites us to explore what we need to release and let go of in order to stay in alignment with our intentions. Eclipse energy amplifies the intensity of the full Moon.

This is our first eclipse on the Pisces/Virgo axis. We are exploring improvement versus our discontent and looking at which patterns need to be disrupted and reordered for us to create something new and better.

Gate 36 is where the potential for miracles lives in the chart. This energy invites us into an exploration of what else is possible. We can defy old patterns and stretch the limits of the human story and condition when this powerful, transformational energy is at play.

With the full Moon being amplified with the intensity of the eclipse, we are untangling ourselves from old patterns that are keeping us from moving forward. Mindset, the willingness to be unrelenting in our authentic self-expression, our deep connection to Source, and our faith are all components that support us in harnessing the power of miracles in the face of an uncertain outcome.

But miracles don't happen without alignment and preparing the way. A miracle isn't simply a serendipitous event. It is preceded by faith and a willingness to suspend all conditioned expectations. This full Moon invites us to cultivate the frequency of faith, to fan the flames of passion and potential and to consciously call in the energy necessary to release ourselves from the shackles and patterns of the path. What old ideas and patterns do you need to release in order to be prepared for something new, something better?

CHALLENGE:

To not let boredom cause you to leap into chaos. To learn to stick with something long enough to become masterful and to bear the fruits of your experience.

OPTIMAL EXPRESSION:

The ability to hold a vision and sustain it with an aligned frequency of emotional energy and to bring the vision into form when the timing is right. It is the ability to stretch the boundaries of the story of humanity by breaking patterns. It is creating miracles through emotional alignment.

UNBALANCED EXPRESSION:

Not waiting for the right timing and leaping into new opportunities without waiting for alignment, causing chaos. To leap from opportunity to opportunity without waiting to see how the story will play out and never getting to experience the full fruition of the experience.

CONTEMPLATIONS:

How does boredom impact my life?

What do I do when I feel bored?

What can I do to keep myself aligned even when I'm bored?

What stories have I experienced that have shattered old patterns and expectations?

How have my stories changed or inspired others?

What do I do to maintain or sustain emotional alignment?

What do I need to add to my daily practice to amp up my emotional energy around my intentions?

AFFIRMATION:

My experiences and stories break old patterns and push the boundaries of the edge of what is possible for humanity. I defy the patterns, and I create miracles through my emotional alignment with possibility. I hold my vision and maintain my emotional energy as I wait to bear the fruit of my intentions and visions.

SEPTEMBER 21, 2024
GATE 46: EMBODIMENT

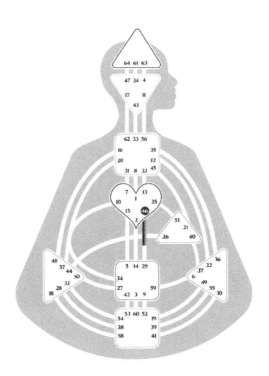

CHALLENGE:

To learn to love your body. To learn to fully be in your body. To learn to love the sensual nature of your physical form and to move it with love and awareness.

JOURNAL QUESTIONS:

Do I love my body?

What can I do to deepen my love for my body?

What parts of my body do I love and appreciate?

Make a list of every part of my body that I love.

What do I need to do to amplify the Life Force I am experiencing in my body?

What kinds of devotion and commitment do I experience that help me harness greater amounts of Life Force in my body?

How can I deepen my commitment and devotion to my body?

AFFIRMATION:

My body is the vehicle for my soul. My ability to fully express who I am (and my life and soul purpose) is deeply rooted in my body's ability to carry my soul. I love, nurture, and commit to my body. I appreciate all of its miraculous abilities and form. Every day I love my body more.

EFT SETUP:

Even though it is hard for me to love my body, I now choose to embrace my amazing physical form and honor it for all the good it brings me, and I deeply and completely love and accept myself.

EARTH:

Gate 25: Spirit

Do you have a regular practice that connects you to Source? How can you deepen this practice this week?

SEPTEMBER 26, 2024
GATE 18: REALIGNMENT

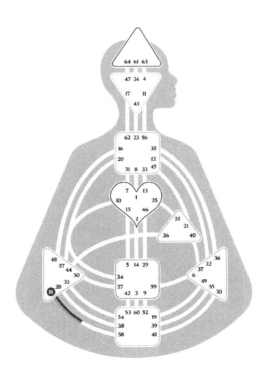

 CHALLENGE:

To learn to wait for the right timing and the right circumstances to offer your intuitive insights into how to fix or correct a pattern. To wait for the right time and the right reason to share your critique. To understand that the purpose of realignment is to create more joy, not to be "right."

 JOURNAL QUESTIONS:

What does joy mean to me? How do I serve it? How do I cultivate joy in my own life?

How does it feel to be "right" about something and keep it to myself?

Do I need to release any old stories about needing to be right?

Do I trust my own insights? Do I have the courage to share them when it is necessary?

AFFIRMATION:

I am a powerful force that realigns patterns. My insights and awareness give people the information they need to deepen their expertise and to experience greater joy. I serve joy and I align the patterns of the world to increase the world's potential for living in the flow of joy.

EFT SETUP:

Even though I feel criticized and judged, I now choose to hear the wisdom of the correction and release my personal attachment, and I deeply and completely love and accept myself.

EARTH:

Gate 17: Anticipation

What do you need to do to release any doubts and fears you may have about your own ability? What accomplishments do you have that you can celebrate and acknowledge?

OCTOBER 2, 2024
GATE 48: WISDOM

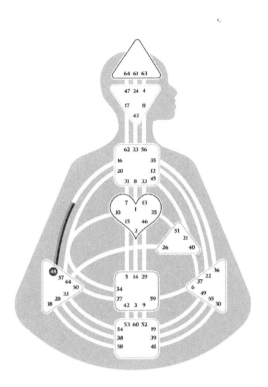

CHALLENGE:

To allow yourself to trust that you will know what you need to know when you need to know it. To not let the fear of not knowing stop you from creating. To not let not knowing hold you back.

JOURNAL QUESTIONS:

Do I trust my own knowing?

What needs to be healed, released, aligned, and brought to my awareness for me to deepen my self-trust?

What practice do I have that keeps me connected to the wisdom of Source?

How can I deepen my connection to Source?

AFFIRMATION:

I am a depth of wisdom and knowledge. My studies and experiences have taught me everything I need to know. I push beyond the limits of my earthly knowledge and take great leaps of faith as a function of my deep connection to Source knowing that I will always know what I need to know when I need to know it.

EFT SETUP:

Even though I am afraid I am not ready to, I now choose to courageously dive in and just do it, and I deeply and completely love and accept myself.

EARTH:

Gate 21: Self-Regulation

How can you be more generous with yourself this week? How can you create an inner and outer environment that is more self-generous?

OCTOBER 2, 2024
NEW MOON/ SOLAR ECLIPSE

 Libra 10 degrees, 02 minutes
Gate 48: The Gate of Wisdom

New Moon energy invites us to explore how we can deepen our alignment with our intentions and asks us to focus on what we want to grow and expand on in our lives. A Solar eclipse signifies new beginnings. Not only this, but the Solar eclipse exposes all that is hidden and not visible. The eclipse also marks an end to what has already ended. Thus, during this eclipse, many of you who did not get closure from events of the past will eventually find total closure.

The theme of this new Moon and Solar eclipse is readiness. We've done our homework. We've gone to the depth with our studies, learning, experience, and understanding. We've trained. We are ready. This powerful energy invites us to untangle ourselves from the fear that the past will repeat itself, from our fears of inadequacy, and from our self-doubt so that we can be prepared for something new.

All of the work that you've done over the past year has given you the foundation of a new story and the capacity to build a new reality. With intentional self-regulation and with a clear set of values and what is truly valuable, we are able to finally begin anew with momentum and clarity. It's time to celebrate our resilience and strength and strike a balance between finishing up our inner healing and committing to a vision for the future. Take time today to acknowledge what has come before and where we're headed.

In the shadow of this energy, we fail to move forward, and we let fear win. We hold ourselves back, over-analyzing. We try to control ourselves and each other as a way of managing fear.

The only way through it is through it. We are being called to acknowledge the fear but to no longer let it block our joy.

CHALLENGE:

To allow yourself to trust that you will know what you need to know when you need to know it. To not let the fear of not knowing stop you from creating. To not let not knowing hold you back.

OPTIMAL EXPRESSION:

The wisdom to explore and learn the depth of knowledge necessary to create a strong foundation for action and mastery. To cultivate your trust in your ability to know how to know and your connection to Source as the true source of your knowledge.

UNBALANCED EXPRESSION:

Paralysis in inadequacy. To be afraid to try something new or go beyond your comfort zone because you think you don't know or are not ready.

CONTEMPLATIONS:

Do I trust my own knowing?

What needs to be healed, released, aligned, and brought to my awareness for me to deepen my self-trust?

What practice do I have that keeps me connected to the wisdom of Source?

How can I deepen my connection to Source??

AFFIRMATION:

I am a depth of wisdom and knowledge. My studies and experiences have taught me everything I need to know. I push beyond the limits of my earthly knowledge and take great leaps of faith as a function of my deep connection to Source, knowing that I will always know what I need to know when I need to know it.

OCTOBER 8, 2024
GATE 57: INSTINCT

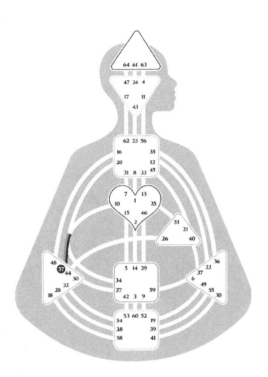

 CHALLENGE:

To learn to trust your own insights and gut. To learn to tell the difference between an instinctive response versus a fear of the future. To become skilled at your connection to your sense of right timing.

 JOURNAL QUESTIONS:

Do I trust my intuition?

What does my intuition feel like to me?

Sometimes doing a retrospective analysis of my intuition/instinct makes it more clear how my intuitive signal works. What experiences in the past have I had that I knew I should or shouldn't do?

How have I experienced my intuition in the past?

When I think about moving forward in my life, do I feel afraid?

What am I afraid of? What can I do to mitigate the fear?

What impulses am I experiencing that are telling me to prepare for what is next in my life?

Am I acting on my impulses? Why or why not?

AFFIRMATION:

My inner wisdom is deeply connected to the pulse of Divine timing. I listen to my inner wisdom and follow my instinct. I know when and how to prepare the way for the future. I take guided action and I trust myself and Source.

EFT SETUP:

Even though it is scary to trust my gut, I now choose to honor my awareness, quiet my mind, and go with what feels right, and I deeply and completely love and accept myself.

EARTH:

Gate 51: Initiation

What lessons have unexpected events brought into your life? Make note of how resilient you are.

OCTOBER 14, 2024
GATE 32: ENDURANCE

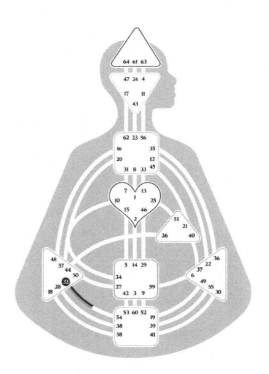

CHALLENGE:

To trust in Divine timing. To prepare for the next step of manifestation and to align with the unfolding of the process. To be patient.

JOURNAL QUESTIONS:

What do I need to do to be prepared to manifest my vision?

What actionable steps need to be completed in order for me to be ready when the timing is right?

What do I need to do to cultivate patience?

Do I have a fear of failing that is causing me to avoid being prepared?

Am I overdoing and being overly prepared?

Am I pushing too hard?

What can I let go of?

AFFIRMATION:

I am a Divine translator for Divine inspiration. I sense and know what needs to be prepared on the earthly plane in order to be ready for right timing. I am aligned with right timing, and I prepare and wait patiently knowing that when the time is right, I am ready to do the work to help transform pain into power.

EFT SETUP:

Even though I have worked hard to make my dreams come true and nothing has happened yet, I trust in Divine timing and keep tending to my vision, and I deeply and completely love and accept myself.

EARTH:

Gate 42: Conclusion

To get the most of this week, explore what unfinished business you need to bring to a conclusion. Are there things you need to say? Situations you need to end and be done with? Endings make room for new beginnings.

OCTOBER 17, 2024
FULL MOON

Aries 24 degrees, 34 minutes

Gate 42: The Gate of Conclusion

Full Moon energy invites us to explore what we need to release and let go of in order to stay in alignment with our intentions.

We cannot control time and timing, but we can influence it. It is natural, as we begin to experience the feeling of momentum and a surge forward, to want to push and rush ahead. When we push against right timing, we run the risk of returning to a state of burnout and depletion. This is not a time to force things into being, but rather to set the stage and be prepared for the natural progression of things.

This full Moon reminds us that we can influence time and timing when we make sure that we take care of any unfinished business. Are there bills that have been ignored that need to be paid? Difficult conversations that need to be had? Anything that's been left undone that needs to be tackled? This is the time to do it!

When we create space by finishing off the old, we signal to the Universe that we're ready. The more ready we are, the easier and speedier it is for new opportunities to find us.

In addition, we are being called to literally set the stage for what's next. We're starting on a new journey. It takes planning, readiness, and, most of all, endurance. Check your mindset. Make sure you haven't put off the things you need to do to lay the foundation for your dreams. Don't let your fear of failure cause you to sabotage your efforts!

CHALLENGE:

To learn to bring things to completion. To allow yourself to be led to where you need to be to finish things. To value your ability to know how to finish and to learn to give up your need to try to start everything. To finish things in order to create space for something new.

OPTIMAL EXPRESSION:

The ability to respond to being inserted into opportunities, experiences, and events that you have the wisdom to facilitate and complete. To know exactly what needs to be completed to create the space for something new.

UNBALANCED EXPRESSION:

Pressure, confusion, and self-judgment for being unable to get things started. Avoiding or putting off things that need to be completed; creating a backlog of projects that can lead to paralysis and overwhelm. Finishing things prematurely due to pressure.

CONTEMPLATIONS:

Do I own and value my natural gift of knowing how to bring things to completion?

What things in my life do I need to finish to make room for something new?

Am I holding on to old circumstances and patterns because I'm afraid to let them go?

Do I judge myself for not starting things?

How can I learn to be gentler with myself?

AFFIRMATION:

I am gifted at knowing when and how to finish things. I respond by bringing events, experiences, and relationships to a conclusion in order to create space for something new and more abundant. I can untangle the cosmic entanglements that keep people stuck in old patterns. My ability to realign and complete things helps others create space for transformation and expansion.

OCTOBER 19, 2024
GATE 50: NURTURING

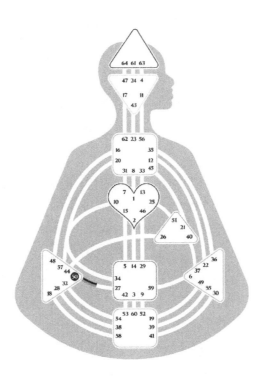

 CHALLENGE:

To learn to transcend guilt and unhealthy obligations that keep you from doing what you need to do to take care of yourself in order to better serve others. To hold to rigid principles to judge others.

 JOURNAL QUESTIONS:

How do I feel about taking care of myself first?

How do I sustain my nurturing energy?

What role does guilt play in driving or motivating me?

What would I choose if I could remove the guilt?

Do I have nonnegotiable values? What are they?

How do I handle people who share different values from me?

AFFIRMATION:

My presence brings love into the room. I nurture and love others. I take care of myself first in order to be better able to serve love. I intuitively know what people need and I facilitate for them a state of self-love and self-empowerment by helping them align more deeply with the power of love. I let go and I allow others to learn from what I model and teach. I am a deep well of love that sustains the planet.

EFT SETUP:

Even though it is hard for me to give and receive love, I now choose to be completely open to receiving and sharing deep and unconditional love starting by deeply and completely loving and accepting myself first.

EARTH:

Gate 3: Innovation

What is working in your life? Take some time to contemplate what aspects of your current reality you'd love to grow and expand upon.

OCTOBER 25, 2024
GATE 28: ADVENTURE/CHALLENGE

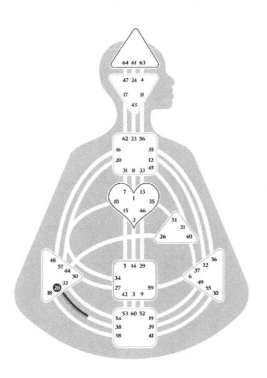

 CHALLENGE:

To not let struggle and challenge leave you feeling defeated and despairing. To learn to face life as an adventure. Do not let challenge and struggle cause you to feel as if you have failed.

 JOURNAL QUESTIONS:

How can I turn my challenge into adventure?

Where do I need to cultivate a sense of adventure in my life?

What do I need to do to rewrite the story of my "failures?"

What meanings, blessings, and lessons have I learned from my challenges?

What needs to be healed, released, aligned, and brought to my awareness for me to trust myself and my choices?

What do I need to do to forgive myself for my perceived past failures?

AFFIRMATION:

I am here to push the boundaries of life and what is possible. I thrive in situations that challenge me. I am an explorer on the leading edge of consciousness and my job is to test how far I can go. I embrace challenge. I am an adventurer. I share all I have learned from my challenges with the world. My stories help give people greater meaning, teach them what is truly worthy of creating, and inspire people to transform.

EFT SETUP:

Even though everything feels hard, I now trust that I am learning what is truly important in my life. I trust the lessons the Universe brings me, and I deeply and completely love and accept myself.

EARTH:

Gate 27: Accountability

Are you taking responsibility for things that aren't yours? Whose problem is it? Can you return the responsibility for the problem back to its rightful owner?

OCTOBER 31, 2024
GATE 44: TRUTH

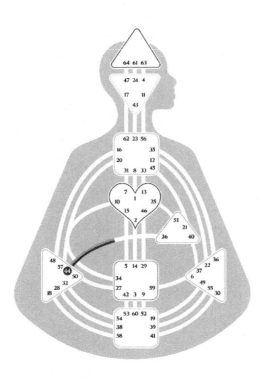

CHALLENGE:

To not get stuck in past patterns. To cultivate the courage to go forward without being stuck in the fear of the past. To learn how to transform pain into power and to have the courage to express your authentic self without compromising or settling.

JOURNAL QUESTIONS:

What patterns from the past are holding me back from moving forward with courage?

Do I see how my experiences from the past have helped me learn more about Who I Truly Am?

What have I learned about my value and my power?

What needs to be healed, released, aligned, and brought to my awareness for me to fully activate my power?

What needs to be healed, released, aligned, and brought to my awareness for me to step boldly into my aligned and authentic path?

AFFIRMATION:

I am powerfully intuitive and can sense the patterns that keep others stuck in limiting beliefs and constricted action. Through my insights and awareness, I help others break free from past limiting patterns and learn to find the power in their pain, find the blessings in their challenges, and help them align more deeply with an authentic awareness of their true value and purpose.

EFT SETUP:

Even though it is hard for me to let go, I deeply and completely love and accept myself.

Even though I am afraid to repeat the past, I now move forward with confidence trusting that I have learned what I needed to learn. I can create whatever future I desire, and I deeply and completely love and accept myself.

EARTH:

Gate 24: Blessings

Take some time to contemplate the hidden blessings in the painful events of the past. Can you find the bigger reason for why you've gone through what you've gone through?

NOVEMBER 1, 2024
NEW MOON

 Scorpio 9 degrees, 34 minutes

Gate 44: The Gate of Truth

New Moon energy invites us to explore how we can deepen our alignment with our intentions and asks us to focus on what we want to grow and expand on in our lives.

This Lunar cycle, starting with the new Moon, calls for us to release and let go of all the old patterns, situations, and habits that might be keeping us from moving forward. The new Moon invites us to explore the fear that the patterns of the past might repeat themselves.

If you go into a forest and you see a bear, it's healthy and natural to run from the bear. If you go into a forest a year later and there is no bear, but you refuse to go in, just in case there is one, you are reacting instead of creating with deliberation. This new Moon invites you into the forest to realize that there is no bear and that the fear of the metaphorical bear is keeping you from enjoying the beauty of the forest.

We often react to life as a low-grade self-protection mechanism. Most of us learn from life that it's not okay or even safe for us to be who we are and how we are. When we internalize this story, we go through our lives hiding and reacting to the possibility that others may judge us or devalue our existence. This new Moon wants you to stop hiding out as a way of protecting yourself. The light of the Moon gives you a clear path and a deep invitation to reveal your authentic self to the world and to heal any place where you've internalized the story that it's not okay for you to be who you are or how you are.

Remember, you are a once-in-a-lifetime cosmic event!

CHALLENGE:

To not get stuck in past patterns. To cultivate the courage to go forward without being stuck in fear of the past. To learn how to transform pain into power and to have the courage to express your authentic self without compromise or settling.

OPTIMAL EXPRESSION:

The ability to see patterns that have created pain and to bring awareness to help yourself and others break old patterns and transform pain into an increased sense of value and alignment with purpose.

UNBALANCED EXPRESSION:

Fear and paralysis that the past patterns are insurmountable and doomed to repeat themselves.

CONTEMPLATIONS:

What patterns from the past are holding me back from moving forward with courage?

Do I see how my experiences from the past have helped me learn more about who I truly am?

What have I learned about my value and my power?

What needs to be healed, released, aligned, and brought to my awareness to fully activate my power?

What needs to be healed, released, aligned, and brought to my awareness to step boldly into my aligned and authentic path?

AFFIRMATION:

I am powerfully intuitive and can sense the patterns that keep others stuck in limiting beliefs and constricted action. Through my insights and awareness, I help others break free from past limiting patterns and learn to find the power in their pain, find the blessings in their challenges, and help them align more deeply with an authentic awareness of their true value and purpose.

NOVEMBER 5, 2024
GATE 1: PURPOSE

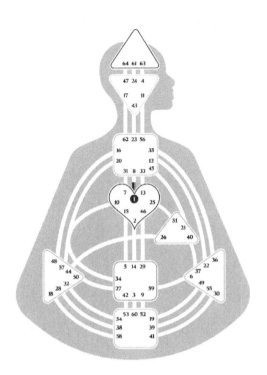

CHALLENGE:

To discover a personal, meaningful, and world-changing narrative that aligns with a sense of purpose and mission. To learn to love yourself enough to honor the idea that your life is the canvas, and you are the artist. To remember that what you create with your life is the contribution you give the world.

JOURNAL QUESTIONS:

Am I fully expressing my authentic self?

What needs to be healed, released, aligned, or brought to my awareness for me to deeply express my authentic self?

Where am I already expressing who I am?

Where have I settled or compromised? What needs to change?

Do I feel connected to my Life Purpose? What do I need to do to deepen that connection?

AFFIRMATION:

My life is an integral part of the cosmos and the Divine Plan. I honor my life and know that the full expression of who I am is the purpose of my life. The more I am who I am, the more I create a frequency of energy that supports others in doing the same. I commit to exploring all of who I am.

EFT SETUP:

Even though I am afraid that I am failing my life mission, I now choose to relax and allow my life to unfold before me with ease and grace. I trust that every step I take is perfectly aligned with my soul purpose, and I deeply and completely love and accept myself.

EARTH:

Gate 2: Allowing

How much good are you willing to allow into your life? Do you believe you can be fully supported?

NOVEMBER 11, 2024
GATE 43: INSIGHT

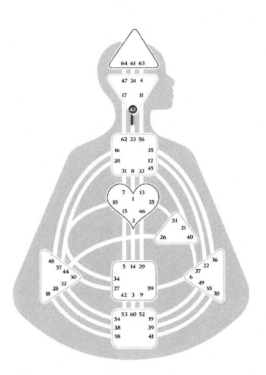

CHALLENGE:

To be comfortable and to trust epiphanies and deep inner knowing, without doubting what you know. To trust that when the timing is right you will know how to share what you know and serve your role as a transformative messenger who has insights that can change the way people think and what they know.

JOURNAL QUESTIONS:

Do I trust in Divine timing?

Do I trust myself and my own inner knowing?

What can I do to deepen my connection with my source of knowing?

What needs to be healed, released, aligned, or brought to my awareness for me to trust my own inner knowing?

AFFIRMATION:

I am a vessel of knowledge and wisdom that has the ability to transform the way people think. I share my knowledge with others when they are ready and vibrationally aligned with what I have to share. When the time is right, I have the right words, and the right insights to help others expand their thinking, recalibrate their mindset, and discover the elegant solutions to the challenges facing humanity.

EFT SETUP:

Even though it is hard to wait for someone to ask me for my insights, I now choose to wait and know that my thoughts are valuable and precious. I only share them with people who value my insights, and I deeply and completely love and accept myself.

EARTH:

Gate 23: Transmission

Take stock of all the times you "knew" something even though you didn't know how you knew. Keep a running list of all your intuitive hits. Start affirming for yourself how reliable your knowingness is.

NOVEMBER 15, 2024
FULL MOON

 Taurus 24 degrees, 0 minutes
Gate 23: The Gate of Transmission

This full Moon offers us an invitation to trust our own inner knowing and to, ultimately, take leadership with what we know. This act of self-trust requires of us tremendous courage because when we operate at this level of deep, intuitive knowing, we don't always have the logical proof of what we know is true. We simply know.

This same energy brings transformation and change in the way we think. We are shifting and changing our mindset and the way in which we process information. As we change our thinking, we come to new conclusions. These new conclusions form the construct of a new way of perceiving and seeing the world. We enter into this new Moon cycle with fresh eyes and a willingness to try something new.

In the shadow of this energy, we are confronted with the unreasonable objections from others or from within ourselves. There is no need for you to prove what you know. This is an exquisite invitation to allow yourself to simply know what you know and to learn to trust that you'll know what you know when you need to know it.

What new things and thoughts are you wanting to create? This is the time to be a steward for new ideas and possibilities and to have the courage to trust yourself.

CHALLENGE:

To recognize that change and transformation are inevitable. To know what needs to happen next and to have to wait for the right timing and the right people to share your insights with. To not jump the gun and try to convince people to understand what you know. To not let yourself slip into negativity and despair when people aren't ready.

OPTIMAL EXPRESSION:

The ability to translate transformative insights with people that offers them a way to transform the way they think. To share what you know with awareness of right timing and to trust your knowingness as an expression of your connection to Source.

UNBALANCED EXPRESSION:

The need to be right. An anxiety or pressure to share what you know with people who aren't ready and then to feel despair or bitterness that they don't understand things the way you do.

CONTEMPLATIONS:

How can I strengthen my connection to Source?

Do I trust what I know?

What comes up for me when I know something, but I don't know how I know what I know?

How do I handle myself when I know something but the people around me aren't ready to hear it yet?

AFFIRMATION:

I change the world with what I know. My insights and awareness have the ability to transform the way people think and perceive the world. I know my words are powerful and transformative. I trust that the people who are ready for the change that I bring will ask me for what I know. I am a vessel for my knowingness, and I nurture myself while I wait to share what I know.

NOVEMBER 16, 2024
GATE 14: CREATION

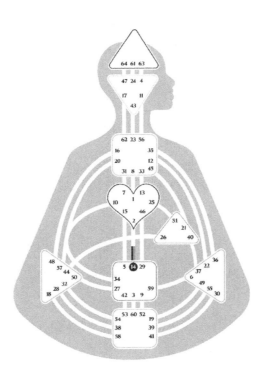

CHALLENGE:

To learn to trust to respond to opportunities that bring resources instead of forcing them or overworking. To learn to value resources and to appreciate how easily they can be created when you are aligned. To be gracious and grateful and not take for granted the resources you have.

JOURNAL QUESTIONS:

Do I trust that I am supported?

Am I doing my "right" work?

What is the work that feels aligned with my purpose?

How is that work showing up in my life right now?

What resources do I have right now that I need to be grateful for?

If I didn't need the money, what work would I be doing?

AFFIRMATION:

I am in the flow of Divine support. When I trust the generous nature of the Divine and I cultivate a state of faith, I receive all the opportunities and support that I need to evolve my life and transform the world. I know that the right work shows up for me, and I am fulfilled in the expression of my life force energy.

EFT SETUP:

Even though I am afraid that I cannot do what I love and make money, I deeply and completely love and accept myself.

EARTH:

Gate 8: Fulfillment

What would your life be like if you felt relentlessly authentic? Do one thing this week that is an authentic expression of who you are, without apology. Be bold.

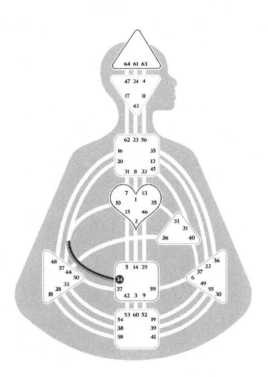

CHALLENGE:

To learn to measure out energy in order to stay occupied and busy but to not burn yourself out trying to force the timing or the "rightness" of a project. To wait to know which project or creation to implement based on when you get something to respond to.

JOURNAL QUESTIONS:

Do I trust in Divine timing?

What do I need to do to deepen my trust?

How do I cultivate greater patience in my life?

What fears come up for me when I think of waiting?

How can I learn to wait with greater faith and ease?

What do I do to occupy myself while I'm waiting?

AFFIRMATION:

I am a powerful servant of Divine timing. When the timing is right, I unify the right people around the right idea and create transformation on the planet. My power is more active when I allow the Universe to set the timing. I wait. I am patient. I trust.

EFT SETUP:

Even though I am afraid to be powerful, I now choose to fully step into my power and allow the Universe to serve me while I serve it, and I deeply and completely love and accept myself.

EARTH:

Gate 20: Patience

How do you manage the pressure you feel around the need for action? What are constructive ways that you can bring yourself into harmony with right timing? What do you do while you're waiting for the timing to align?

NOVEMBER 26, 2024—DECEMBER 15, 2024
MERCURY RETROGRADE

Gate 26: The Gate of Integrity
Gate 5: The Gate of Consistency
Gate 9: The Gate of Convergence

Retrograde cycles encourage us to go inward to explore the themes the planets give us. Mercury is the planet associated with communication. When Mercury goes retrograde it gives us an opportunity to go inward and contemplate how we can better align ourselves to have greater influence and impact in the world. Take your time to find the right words during this cycle. Do your best to not make big decisions, sign contracts, or make large purchases. Expect delays. Breathe and be patient with others.

This retrograde cycle reminds us that we create more expansion and resources when we choose in integrity with our self-worth. If we don't value ourselves, we run the risk of creating when we are out of integrity, putting us at risk for physical illness, a misuse of our physical resources—including money, immoral choices, actions that compromise our authentic identity or overcommit energy—that we don't have.

Mercury reminds us that to live in alignment with our value we need to consistently focus on what we want and who we are. We need consistent habits that keep us rooted in who we are. We need time to focus without distraction on where we're headed, the power of our dreams, and the importance of our purpose.

Take some time during these works to explore your habits. Are you doing what you need to do to stay in integrity with yourself, your work, your commitments, even with others? Spend time in silence and really connect with yourself and that once-in-lifetime cosmic event that is YOU!

CHALLENGE:

To discover where you may have breaches in integrity and readjust your life and habits to help you realign with your self-worth, your purpose, and your right place in the world.

OPTIMAL EXPRESSION:

To deepen your practice of focus and to use this focus to cultivate habits and ways of being that enhance your connection to your value and the unique role in the world that only you can play! To be relentlessly aligned with your authentic self. To ensure that every choice you make is in alignment with your purpose and mission.

UNBALANCED EXPRESSION:

To create out of integrity in an attempt to prove your value. To try to overcompensate for your perceived lack of value by pushing too hard and burning yourself out.

CONTEMPLATIONS:

Do I value myself?

Do I proclaim my authentic identity to the world?

Do I take care of my body?

Do I take care of my money and other physical resources?

Do I compromise my authentic self?

Do I resort to immoral choices because I'm afraid I won't get my fair share?

Do I commit energy I don't have in order to be liked or valued by others?

What needs to change?

AFFIRMATION:

I am an irreplaceable part of the cosmic plan. The Universe literally is what it is today because of me. I have a vital role to play in life and I'm so valuable that no one else but me can fulfill this role. I nurture myself. I value myself. I take care of my body, my money, my authentic identity, and my energy as a way of sustaining myself. I trust that when I proclaim and defend my value, all good things come to me.

NOVEMBER 28, 2024
GATE 9: CONVERGENCE

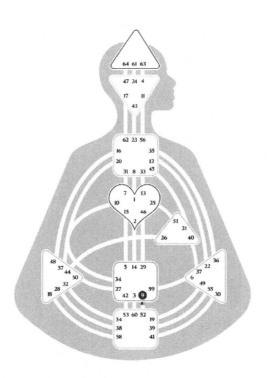

CHALLENGE:

The energy is about learning where to place your focus. When we work with the energy of this gate, we have to learn to see the trees AND the forest. This gate can make us seem blind to the big picture and we can lose our focus by getting stuck going down a rabbit hole.

JOURNAL QUESTIONS:

Where am I putting my energy and attention? Is it creating the growth I am seeking?

What do I need to focus on?

Is my physical environment supporting my staying focused?

Do I have a practice that supports me sustaining my focus? What can I do to increase my focus?

AFFIRMATION:

I place my focus and attention on the details that support my creative manifestation. I am clear. I easily see the parts of the whole, and I know exactly what to focus on to support my evolution and the evolution of the world.

EFT SETUP:

Even though I have been frustrated with my lack of focus, I now choose to be clear, stay focused, and take the actions necessary to create my intentions, and I deeply and completely love and accept myself.

EARTH:

Gate 16: Zest

Where have you sidelined your enthusiasms because others have told you that you can't do what you dream of doing?

DECEMBER 1, 2024
NEW MOON

 Sagittarius 9 degrees, 32 minutes

Gate 9: The Gate of Convergence

New Moon energy invites us to explore how we can deepen our alignment with our intentions and asks us to focus on what we want to grow and expand on in our lives.

Focus is an essential part of manifesting and creating. If you are distracted and not putting your energy towards what you want to be creating in your life, it's going to take longer for you to actually experience what you're wanting in your physical world. This full Moon invites you to explore what you are focusing on and where you are putting your creative attention. Are your efforts creating what you want, or do you need to refocus in order to create more fulfillment?

We were initiated in this Lunar cycle with new ideas and new ways of thinking about things. If we are not focusing forward, or putting our attention on the past, it makes it hard for us to gain traction and momentum. Are you giving your new way of thinking and your new perspective the attention it needs to take root in your life? What needs to shift? How can you clear your life from distractions and place your focus on what you really want to create right now?

CHALLENGE:

The energy is about learning where to place your focus. When we work with the energy of this gate, we have to learn to see the trees AND the forest. This gate can make us seem blind to the big picture, and we can lose our focus by getting stuck going down a rabbit hole.

OPTIMAL EXPRESSION:

The ability to see the big picture and prioritize where to focus your energy.

UNBALANCED EXPRESSION:

Feeling pressured to figure out where to place your focus. Feeling overwhelmed and confused by too many options and choices. Not being able to see the relationship between ideas and actions and missing the essential details.

CONTEMPLATIONS:

Where am I putting my energy and attention?

Is it creating the growth that I'm seeking?

What do I need to focus on?

Is my physical environment supporting staying focused?

Do I have a practice that supports me in sustaining my focus?

What can I do to increase my focus?

AFFIRMATION:

I place my focus and attention on the details that support my creative manifestation. I am clear. I quickly see the parts of the whole, and I know precisely what to focus on to support my evolution and the evolution of the world.

DECEMBER 3, 2024
GATE 5: CONSISTENCY

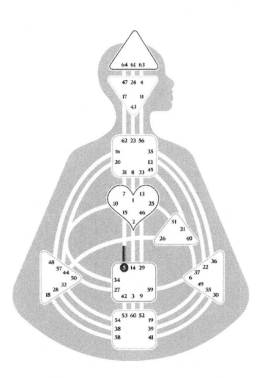

 CHALLENGE:

To learn to craft order, habits, and rhythm that support alignment, connection, and the flow of Life Force energy and the fulfillment of purpose. To become skilled at staying in tune with consistent habits and alignment that support your growth and evolution no matter what is going on around you. Aligning with natural order and staying attuned to the unfolding of the flow of the natural world.

 JOURNAL QUESTIONS:

What do I need to do to create habits that fuel my energy and keep me vital and feeling connected to myself and Source?

What habits do I have that might not be serving my highest expression? How can I change those habits?

What kind of environment do I need to cultivate to support my rhythmic nature?

AFFIRMATION:

Consistency gives me power. When I am aligned with my own natural rhythm and the rhythm of life around me, I cultivate strength and connection with Source, and I am a beacon of stability and order. The order I hold is the touchstone, the returning point of love, that is sustained through cycles of change. The rhythms I maintain set the standard for compassionate action in the world.

EFT SETUP:

Even though I feel nervous/scared/worried about waiting for Divine Timing, I now choose to create habits that support my connection with Source while I wait, and I deeply and completely love and accept myself.

EARTH:

Gate 35: Experience

What experiences and stories from your own life do you have to share with others? Write a story about one of your favorite adventures you've experienced in your life. What did you learn? How has that shaped who you are?

DECEMBER 9, 2024
GATE 26: INTEGRITY

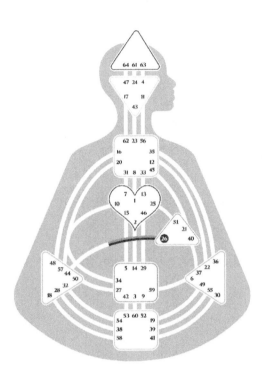

 CHALLENGE:

To learn to take your right place and embody your value enough to act as if you are precious. To heal past traumas and elevate your self-worth. To trust in support enough to do the right thing and to nurture yourself so that you have more to give.

 JOURNAL QUESTIONS:

Where might I be experiencing a breach in my moral identity, physical, resource, or energy integrity?

What do I need to do to bring myself back into integrity?

When I act without integrity, can it be traumatic?

What trauma do I have that I need to heal?

How can I rewrite that story of my trauma as an initiation back into my true value?

What do I need to do right now to nurture myself and to replenish my value?

AFFIRMATION:

I am a unique, valuable, and irreplaceable part of the cosmic plan. I am always supported in fulfilling my right place. I take care of my body, my energy, my values, and my resources so that I have more to share with the world. I claim and defend my value and fully live in the story of who I am with courage.

EFT SETUP:

Even though I am afraid to share my truth, I now choose to speak it clearly and confidently, and I deeply and completely love and accept myself.

EARTH:

Gate 45: Distribution

This is a vital week to focus on what gifts you have to share with the world. How can you learn to give more without burning yourself out or martyring yourself? What do you need to do to increase your capacity to give and share?

DECEMBER 14, 2024
GATE 11: THE CONCEPTUALIST

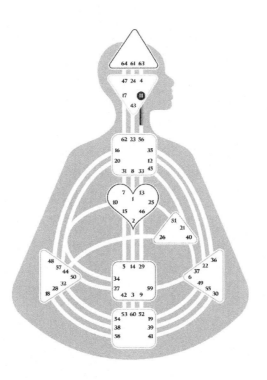

CHALLENGE:

To sort through and manage all the ideas and inspiration you hold. To trust that the ideas that are yours will show up for you in an actionable way. To value yourself enough to trust the ideas you have and to wait for the right people to share those ideas with.

JOURNAL QUESTIONS:

What do I do with inspiration when I receive it?

Do I know how to serve as a steward for my ideas? Or do I feel pressure to try to force them into form?

How much do I value myself? Am I valuing my ideas?

Do I trust the Universe? Do I trust that the ideas that are mine to take action on will manifest in my life according to my Human Design Type and Strategy?

What can I do to manage the pressure I feel to manifest my ideas?

Am I trying to prove my value with my ideas?

AFFIRMATION:

I am a Divine vessel of inspiration. Ideas flow to me constantly. I protect and nurture these ideas knowing that my purpose in life is to share ideas and inspiration with others. I use the power of these ideas to stimulate my imagination and the imagination of others. I trust the infinite abundance and alignment of the Universe and I wait for signs to know which ideas are mine to manifest.

EFT SETUP:

Even though I have many ideas, I now trust that I will know exactly what action to take and when to take it, and I deeply and completely love and accept myself.

EARTH:

Gate 12: The Channel

Spend some time this week contemplating what you need to do to deepen your connection with Source. Add some kind of creativity to your play and rest this week.

DECEMBER 15, 2024
FULL MOON

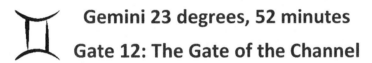 **Gemini 23 degrees, 52 minutes**

Gate 12: The Gate of the Channel

Full Moon energy invites us to explore what we need to release and let go of in order to stay in alignment with our intentions.

For the past few Moon cycles, we've been exploring all the different ways that we know things. We've been learning to trust our intuition, to not lock ourselves into reasoning being the only path to truth, and to tune in to higher sources of information.

This full Moon invites us to go even deeper and to explore and release anything that might be keeping us from trusting our higher ways of knowing. We are sublimely and intricately interwoven into the Cosmic field of life's intelligence. When we live true to ourselves, awakening the feeling of truth in our body and cultivating a deep and devoted relationship with Source, we have access to information that allows us to take quantum leaps of creativity. We see solutions to the challenges facing humanity. We adopt a point of view that is optimistic and faith filled.

But we can't see this if we try to push and force it.

If you try to push your truth out into the world before the timing is right for you to share, you might find that you grapple and are challenged to find the right words. The people around you might struggle to understand exactly what you're trying to share, and you might even feel like no one gets it. Right timing is essential when working with this energy.

You may find that this Moon cycle gives you the final permission you need to speak your truth and to begin building a world rooted in what you know is right for you, even if it is perceived as "unreasonable." Now is the time to call in the courage to be relentlessly authentic and trust that you are deeply and fully supported!

CHALLENGE:

To honor the Self enough to wait for the right time and mood to speak. To know that shyness is actually a signal that the timing isn't right to share your transformational insights and expressions. When the timing is right, to have the courage to share what you feel and sense. To honor the fact that your voice and the words you offer are a direct connection to Source, and you channel the potential for transformation. To own your creative power.

OPTIMAL EXPRESSION:

To know that your voice is an expression of transformation and a vehicle for Divine insight. The words you speak, the insights and creativity you share have the power to change others and the world. This energy is so powerful that people have to be ready to receive it. When you are articulate, then the timing is correct. If you struggle to find the words, have the courage to wait until it feels more aligned. You have a powerful ability to craft language and creative expressions that changes people's perceptions.

UNBALANCED EXPRESSION:

The struggle to try to speak ideas into form when it's not the right time. Letting hesitancy and caution paralyze you. Trying to force ideas and words.

CONTEMPLATIONS:

How has shyness caused me to judge myself?

What do I need to do to cultivate a deeper connection with Source?

What do I need to do to connect more deeply with my creative power?

AFFIRMATION:

I am a creative being. My words, self-expression, and creative offerings have the power to change the way people see and understand the world. I am a vessel of Divine transformation and I serve Source through the words that I share. I wait for the right timing and when I am aligned with timing and flow, my creativity creates beauty and grace in the world. I am a Divine channel and I trust that the words I serve will open the hearts of others.

DECEMBER 20, 2024
GATE 10: SELF-LOVE

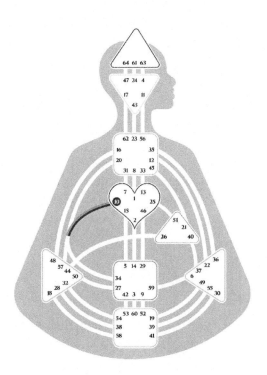

 CHALLENGE:

To learn to love yourself. To learn to take responsibility for your own creations.

 JOURNAL QUESTIONS:

Do I love myself?

What can I do to deepen my self-love?

Where can I find evidence of my lovability in my life right now?

What do I need to do to take responsibility for situations I hate in my life right now? What needs to change?

Where am I holding blame or victimhood in my life? How could I turn that energy around?

AFFIRMATION:

I am an individuated aspect of the Divine. I am born of love. My nature is to love and be loved. I am in the full flow of giving and receiving love. I know that the quality of love that I have for myself sets the direction for what I attract into my life. I am constantly increasing the quality of love I experience and share with the world.

EFT SETUP:

Even though I struggle with loving myself, I now choose to be open to discovering how to love myself anyway, and I deeply and completely love and accept myself.

EARTH:

Gate 15: Compassion

Contemplate what old patterns in your life right now need to be healed and released. Take at least one grounded or symbolic way to commit to shifting and changing these patterns.

DECEMBER 25, 2024
GATE 58: THE GATE OF JOY

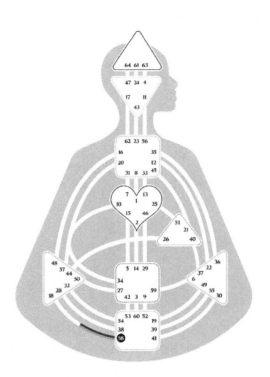

CHALLENGE:

To follow the drive to create the fulfillment of your potential. To learn to craft a talent and make it consummate through joyful learning and repetition. To learn to embrace joy as a vital force of creative power without guilt or denial.

JOURNAL QUESTIONS:

What brings me the greatest joy?

How can I deepen my practice of joy?

How can I create more joy in my life?

What keeps me from fulfilling my potential and my talent?

What am I afraid of?

AFFIRMATION:

I am a consummate curator of my own talent. I use my joy to drive me to embody the fun expression of all that I am. I practice as my path to excellency. I know that from repetition and consistency comes a more skillful expression of my talent. I embrace learning and growing, and I commit to the full expression of my joy.

EFT SETUP:

Even though it is hard to let go of the past, I now choose to release it and embrace all the joy that is available to me right now, and I deeply and completely love and accept myself.

EARTH:

Gate 52: Perspective

Is there anything in your environment or your life that you need to move out of the way for you to deepen your focus?

DECEMBER 30, 2024
NEW MOON

Capricorn 9 degrees, 43 minutes

Gate 58: The Gate of Joy of Mastery

New Moon energy invites us to explore how we can deepen our alignment with our intentions and asks us to focus on what we want to grow and expand on in our lives.

Now that we've been cultivating a deep relationship with our inner knowing, it's time to turn our attention to evolving our "knowingness" into our joy. It's been a year of disruption and upheaval for many of us. The planets have been helping us let go of what no longer serves us. Truths have been revealed. We've been tested and forged. We're strong and more resilient.

We started off the year with an overarching theme that invited us to explore the power of creating from a place of authenticity and an alignment with our true self. This power of alignment has given us a spark of energy and momentum to draw on, even when times have been very challenging.

Now the path is clear and we're ready to set a course for a vision of a new world that is rooted in following that which brings us the greatest joy. In the past, we learned that success and endurance were rooted in hard work, compromise, and settling. This Moon brings us a new way of defining success. We are encouraged and supported by the cosmos to do things that spark our passion and give us joy.

Will there be hard days? Of course. Will there be challenges? For sure. But the joy we've found shines the way forward and we're driven to try, practice, recalibrate, and keep moving forward!

This new Moon invites you to recommit to your joy and to find the dreams and pursuits that spark a quality of joy inside of you that inspires you to keep moving forward, no matter what.

CHALLENGE:

To follow the drive to create the fulfillment of your potential. To learn to craft a talent and make it masterful through joyful learning and repetition. To learn to embrace joy as a vital force of creative power without guilt or denial.

OPTIMAL EXPRESSION:

To harness the joy of becoming masterful and refine your practice until you fulfill your potential. To live in the flow of joy.

UNBALANCED EXPRESSION:

To deny joy. To avoid the practice of mastery. To feel guilty or ashamed to do what you love. To disbelieve in joy.

CONTEMPLATIONS:

What brings me the greatest joy?

How can I deepen my practice of joy?

How can I create more joy in my life?

What keeps me from fulfilling my potential and my talent?

What am I afraid of?

AFFIRMATION:

I am a highly skilled curator of my own talent. I use my joy to drive me to skillfully accomplish the fun expression of all that I am. I practice as my path to my own level of perfection. I know that a more highly skilled level of expression of my talent comes from repetition and consistency. I embrace learning and growing, and I commit to the full expression of my joy.

DECEMBER 31, 2024
GATE 38: THE VISIONARY

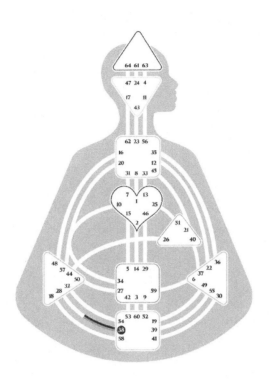

 CHALLENGE:

To experience challenge as a way of knowing what is worth fighting for. To turn the story of struggle into a discovery of meaning and to let the power of what you discover serve as a foundation for a strong vision of transformation that brings dreams into manifested form.

 JOURNAL QUESTIONS:

Do I know what is worth committing to and fighting for in my life?

Do I have a dream that I am sharing with the world?

Do I know how to use my struggles and challenges as the catalyst for creating deeper meaning in the world? In my life?

AFFIRMATION:

My challenges, struggles, and adventures have taught me about what is truly valuable in life. I use my understanding of experiences to hold a vision of what else is possible for the world. I am aligned with the values that reflect the preciousness of life, and I sustain a vision for a world that is aligned with heart. My steadfast commitment to my vision inspires others to join me in creating a world of equitable, sustainable peace.

EFT SETUP:

Even though things seem hard and challenging, I now choose to use my challenges to help me get clear about what I really want, and I deeply and completely love and accept myself.

EARTH:

Gate 39: Recalibration

Where do you need to tweak your perspective to see abundance where you think there is lack? How can you shift the story to see what you have versus what you think you don't? Spend some time practicing reframing your perspective this week.

JANUARY 5, 2025
GATE 54: DIVINE INSPIRATION

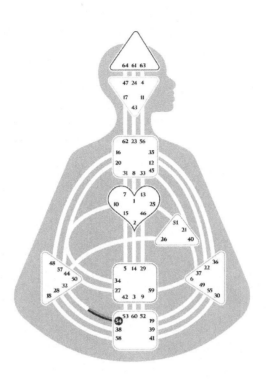

CHALLENGE:

To learn to be a conduit for Divine inspiration. To be patient and to wait for alignment and right timing before taking action. To be at peace with stewardship for ideas and to learn to trust the Divine trajectory of an inspiration.

JOURNAL QUESTIONS:

What do I do to get inspired?

How do I interface with my creative muse?

Is there anything I need to do or prepare in order to be ready for the next step in the manifestation of my dream or inspiration?

How will I know when I am inspired? Will I feel it in my body?

AFFIRMATION:

I am a Divine conduit for inspiration. Through me new ideas about creating sustainability and peace on the planet are born. I tend to my inspirations, give them love and energy, and prepare the way for their manifestations in the material world.

EFT SETUP:

Even though I am afraid my dreams will not come true, I now choose to dream wildly and trust that my dreams will come true. All I have to do is focus my mind, trust and know that all will unfold perfectly, and I deeply and completely love and accept myself.

EARTH:

Gate 53: Starting

What identities and attachments do you have about being the one who starts and finishes something? How can you deepen your trust in right timing?

JANUARY 11, 2025
GATE 61: WONDER

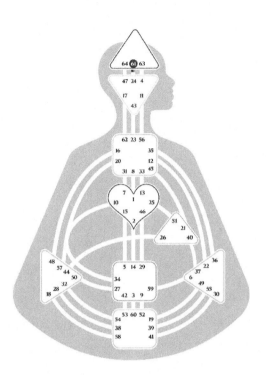

CHALLENGE:

To not get lost in trying to answer or figure out why. To maintain a state of wonder. To not let the pressure of trying to know keep you from being present.

JOURNAL QUESTIONS:

What do I do to maintain my sense of wonder?

How can I deepen my awe of the magnificence of the Universe?

What old thoughts, patterns, and beliefs do I need to release in order to align with my knowingness and to trust my "delusional confidence" as a powerful creative state?

What greater perspectives can I see on the events of my life?

What are the greatest lessons I've learned from my pain?

How do I use these lessons to expand my self-expression?

AFFIRMATION:

I have a direct connection to a cosmic perspective that gives me an expanded view of the meaning of the events in my life and the lives of others. I see the wonder and innocence of life and stay present in a constant state of awe. I am innocent and pure in my understanding of the world and my innocence is the source of my creative alignment.

EFT SETUP:

Even though I do not know all the answers, I now choose to surrender and trust that I am being loved, supported, and nurtured by the infinite, loving Source that is the Universe.

EARTH:

Gate 62: Preparation

This week's mantra: I am prepared. I'll know what I need to know when I need to know it. I know what to prepare when it's time to prepare it. I relax and trust in the flow. Repeat as needed.

JANUARY 13, 2024

FULL MOON

 Cancer 23 degrees, 59 minutes

Gate 62: The Gate of Preparation

Full Moon energy invites us to explore what we need to release and let go of in order to stay in alignment with our intentions.

The energy of 2025 begins with the theme of practicality. This Moon cycle invited us to commit to our joy, now we're working out the details and getting ready to roll our sleeves up and do the work to bring our vision into reality.

This energy invites us to get ready, gather the materials we need, set the stage. It's an exploratory and exciting energy. It's also an energy that begs us to trust the process. We can worry under this influence, but we are remembering the lessons of 2024. We relax knowing that we'll know what we need to know when we need to know it.

This full Moon asks you to explore what needs to be finished up and moved out of the way in order for you to get ready for what's next. This is the final metaphorical housekeeping that you need to tend to before getting traction on a brand-new cycle of expansion.

We made it through the disruptions and the following void. Now it's time to grow!

Take some time under this full Moon to ask yourself what you need to do to be prepared for a year of growth and expansion. What do you need to do to stabilize your mindset and vibration? What practices do you need to strengthen to continue on your path of growth?

CHALLENGE:

To trust that you'll be prepared for the next step. To not let worry and over-preparation detract you from being present to the moment. To let the fear of not being ready keep you trapped.

OPTIMAL EXPRESSION:

The ability to be attuned to what is necessary to be prepared, and trust that your alignment will inform you of everything you need. Being able to relax and trust that you will what you need to know when you need to know it.

UNBALANCED EXPRESSION:

Fear and worry. Over-preparation. Allowing the plan to override the flow.

CONTEMPLATIONS:

Do I worry?

How do I manage my worry?

What can I do to trust that I know what I need to know?

What proof do I have that I am in the flow of preparation?

Is there anything I need to plan for in my life right now?

Am I over-planning?

Does my need for contingency plans keep me stuck?

AFFIRMATION:

I create the foundation for the practice of skillful accomplishment by engineering a plan of action that creates growth. I am in the flow of my understanding, and I use my knowledge and experience to be prepared for the evolution of what's next. I am ready, and I am prepared. I trust my own preparation and allow myself to be in the flow, knowing that I will know what I need to know when I need to know it.

JANUARY 16, 2025
GATE 60: CONSERVATION

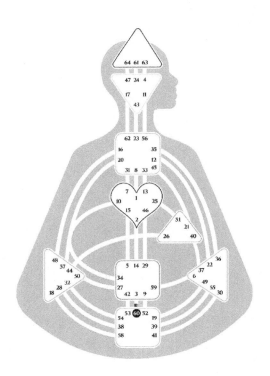

CHALLENGE:

To not let the fear of loss overwhelm your resourcefulness. To learn to find what is working and focus on it instead of looking at the loss and disruption.

JOURNAL QUESTIONS:

What change am I resisting?

What am I afraid of?

What are the things in my life that are working that I need to focus on?

Is my fear of loss holding me back?

AFFIRMATION:

I am grateful for all the transformation and change in my life. I know that disruption is the catalyst for my growth. I am able to find the blessings of the past and incorporate them in my innovative vision for the future. I am optimistic about the future, and I transform the world by growing what works.

EFT SETUP:

Even though it is hard to let go of things that did not work, I now release all the clutter from the past, and I deeply and completely love, accept, and trust myself.

EARTH:

Gate 56: Expansion

Tell yourself a story about your life, your future, and your dreams that causes you to expand energetically. Allow yourself to truly fill up your energy field with expansion.

SUMMARY

Your Quantum Human Design™ is your key to understanding your energy, your life purpose, your life path, and your soul's journey in this lifetime. You are a once-in-a-lifetime cosmic event and the fulfillment of your potential and purpose is the greatest gift you can give the world.

I hope this year has been revolutionary for you and that you reconnected with the true story of who you are and the power and possibility of your very special life.

If you need additional support and resources to help you on your life path and soul's journey, please visit www.quantumalignmentsystem.com, where you can find specialists and practitioners who will help you understand the story of your Human Design chart, coach you, and assist you in getting to the root of any pain, blocks, or limiting beliefs that may be keeping you from enjoying your life story. There are all kinds of free goodies, videos, e-books, and resources to help you on your way!

Thank you again for being YOU! We are who we are because you are who you are!

From my heart to yours,

Karen

ABOUT THE AUTHOR

Karen Curry Parker, PhD is an expert in Quantum Human Design and developed a system to help explore the relationship between quantum physics and Human Design. She's the creator of Quantum Conversations, a successful podcast with over 90,000 downloads in fewer than twelve months, and two systems of Human Design: Quantum Human Design™ and the Quantum Alignment System™. Multiple news outlets, radio shows, and tele-summits have featured her work on their programs.

Karen is also the author of numerous bestselling books all designed to help you create the life you were destined to live and find and embrace the purpose of your existence.

Karen is available for private consultations, keynote talks, and to conduct in-house seminars and workshops.

To run your chart with the new Quantum Human Design language, go to

FreeHumanDesignChart.com

and to find out more about Quantum Alignment visit:

www.quantumalignmentsystem.com

You can reach her at

Karen@quantumalignmentsystem.com

For more great books on Human Design, please visit our online store at books.gracepointpublishing.com

If you enjoyed reading *2024 Quantum Human Design Evolution Guide* and purchased it through an online retailer, please return to the site and write a review to help others find this book.

Printed in Great Britain
by Amazon

38731694R00119